T0149425

The 21ˢᵗ Century Guide to Bachelorhood

Lessons Learned Over the Past 20 Years

BRAD BERKOWITZ

iUniverse, Inc.
New York   Bloomington

The 21st Century Guide to Bachelorhood
Lessons Learned Over the Past 20 Years

iUniverse books may be ordered through booksellers or by contacting:

iUniverse
1663 Liberty Drive
Bloomington, IN 47403
www.iuniverse.com
1-800-Authors (1-800-288-4677)

ISBN: 978-1-4401-1421-2 (pbk)
ISBN: 978-1-4401-1422-9 (ebk)

Library of Congress Control Number: 2009920063

Printed in the United States of America

iUniverse rev. date: 1/6/2009

Contents

I. Introduction

Guys and girls have been trying to better understand each other for decades, however, to no avail. Psychologists undertake massive studies, sociology professors write theses, and television talk show personalities host shows covering the subject, but we are as far away as ever from understanding the opposite sex.

This book will analyze dating and relationships from a male point of view. The information contained will not be a psychological or anatomical study of what differentiates men and women. Instead, it is a practical guide to being a single guy, what we as single men are thinking, and why we do what we do.

The book will begin by shedding light on the different stages of a guy's life after college, and why a guy's social life gets better every year, while a girl's social life usually doesn't. It will then explain some of the best places in your town to meet members of the opposite sex.

The book will continue by explaining the chronological anatomy of a relationship, and what guys are thinking at all stages during the process. It will explain all of the pitfalls and all of the areas where a relationship can end.

It will shed light on what you should avoid during the beginning of the relationship, when to introduce her to your friends, and when she can finally be referred to as your girlfriend.

The next section will explain why blind dates are frequently a waste of your time and money, and how they can actually damage your relationship with the introducing friend. It will discuss all of the thoughts that enter a guy's mind when he is planning the date, what he is thinking when he finally meets the girl, and how he is already mapping out his escape route as soon as he meets her.

The following section will answer all of those interesting questions that girls have concerning guys. You will find out: why guys ask for girls' phone numbers and never call them, why it is more important to men than women to have physically attractive spouses, why men sleep with women and then want to go home, why men dislike shopping, how money affects relationships, why men like to date sluts yet marry "nice" girls, why only unattractive women ask guys out, and why girls always think that their friends are gorgeous.

Finally, the book will analyze the ways guys think. This chapter will discuss: what guys do when they date more than one woman, how guys should use their dogs as chick magnets, why you should never take a date to dinner near your apartment, what guys can do to make themselves more appealing to women, why all men want to be with two women at one time, and why you should always wait before you introduce your girlfriend to your family.

A great deal of what you read in this book will take on a humorous tone, but do not be fooled. The information contained within this book is actually the way guys see the world. It is very different from how girls see it, and they too can learn some very useful things. Read and enjoy.

II. The Stages of Life

Guys and girls go through some very interesting stages in their dating lives. Both sexes experience periods of time in their lives when they have difficulty dating, and both have times when they find it easier to come upon dates. It all has to do with their respective ages and what stage they are in their lives. Sound confusing? Read on.

Senior year in college is a great time to be a guy. While in his senior year, a guy can go out with any girl he wants. The senior girls, who had been in great demand for the past three years, are now desperate for a date or boyfriend. They were used to dating older guys while they were juniors, but now they are forced to date senior guys, or stay at home and take warm, candlelit baths while listening to an Enigma CD. Guys, on the other hand, are at liberty to date a girl from any class. There are four years worth of girls, and all of them want to go out with seniors. The freshman class is new and exciting. The sophomores are available (now that last year's senior guys have graduated), and the juniors are more mature. The senior girls, however, have no choice. There is nobody else at school for them to date. Senior year in college is a great year to be a guy!

Life changes so drastically with respect to dating after you graduate college and enter the real world. Once again, young girls are in demand by older guys in the working world and twenty-two-year-old guys are pond scum. All of the girls that you dated the previous year are still in college, and the girls you associate with now are all older than you. Dating becomes extremely difficult for guys. Girls, however, are mint. Every guy in his mid-twenties is looking at the new crop of girls entering the workplace and salivating. The same girls that you consoled in your senior year at college about not having dates are the girls who now have lots of dates. Now it is your turn to have difficulties finding a girl to date.

As guys get older and more mature emotionally, physically, and professionally, dating becomes so much easier. After you've graduated college, dating gets easier and easier with every year that comes. You gain confidence, learn more about relationships, and begin to meet new girls as they graduate from college. A guy's social life improves as he gets older because the crop of younger talent that wants to go out with him grows bigger and bigger each year. Once he gets into his late twenties and early thirties, a guy has ten years worth of girls from which to choose.

Girls, however, experience a somewhat opposite effect. They become more desirable as they progress into their mid to upper twenties, but that stops pretty quickly as the big 3-0 approaches. Ask any girl about becoming thirty years old, and they will change the subject. Ask any guy about becoming thirty, and he smiles about the party they had in his honor and all of the girls he is dating. Girls dread the coming of their thirtieth birthday and they change once they become thirty. Those not married by their thirtieth birthday can begin to get depressed if they aren't married. They are harassed by their families and begin to think that they may never find Mr. Right, only Mr. Right Now. Girls begin to concentrate more on their careers and try to take the focus off of their stagnant dating lives. Many even buy a dog at or around their thirtieth birthday. When you see a woman with a dog and you think you might be interested in her, go over to her and ask about the dog. Eventually you will find out how old the dog is. Not only will you have a simple way of meeting her, but you can usually find out roughly how old she is by the age of the dog.

Guys in their thirties should date girls between twenty-four and thirty, not girls in their thirties. Girls in their thirties are overly ready to get married, will rush the relationship, and will want to have children the day after they get married because they think their biological clocks are ticking louder than Big Ben (which isn't true). Guys want to date younger girls because they look better (remember that guys are extremely looks conscious) and are not ready to jump the broom (get married) very quickly. A relationship can proceed at a normal pace if you do not date girls in their thirties, unless of course the guy is in his upper thirties or lower to mid-forties, which makes the relationship age appropriate. More and more people are getting married in their thirties, so what is the rush? Don't believe it when girls tell you they have to be married soon because their clocks are running. Bullshit. The only things running are the guys, away from the girls that feed them that crap.

III. Where to Meet Girls

Meeting new girls is a lot of fun and not very difficult. You just have to put yourself in the right place at the right time, and seize the opportunity when it arises. The following are places to meet girls, with an analysis on the merits of each one. Everybody will have places that they prefer, but these seem to be the most popular.

Restaurants are one of the best places to meet girls. You can meet a new girl at the bar before or after dinner, or at the dinner table itself. If you spot a girl during dinner that you would like to meet, make sure that your seat faces her and try to make eye contact. When you do make eye contact, continue to glance at her every once in a while, and watch her reaction. If she smiles back or starts glancing at you, and isn't having dinner with another guy, send her a drink. Casually ask your waiter what she is drinking. Ask him to send her another and to tell her that it was sent to her by you. See what her reaction is. If she smiles and/or toasts you, make sure that you walk over to her table and introduce yourself. Talk to her for about a minute or two, but don't overstay your welcome at the table. After all, she is having dinner with her friend who could now feel neglected. Ask the girl if you could meet her for a drink at the bar after dinner or if you could meet her and her friend at another place after dinner. If not, ask for her business card and tell her that you would like to take her to lunch. In any case, make sure you get her full name and where she works, just in case you don't see her again that night. You can always try to get her number at work from the phone book. Calling her at work is less threatening and she will appreciate the effort you took to get her number.

If the girl is on a date, the situation is more problematic. You may still try to flirt with her, but be careful. She may really like the guy she is with, in which case you will embarrass yourself (or get your ass whipped). The best thing to do in this situation is to try to meet her on the way to the bathroom. Keep in mind that a woman will always go to the ladies room at least once during the meal, so take advantage of the opportunity. Make some interesting conversation en route to the bathroom and try to determine if the guy is her boyfriend. You may even be as bold as to ask her outright. You can usually tell by her mannerisms at the table. If she keeps smiling at you, go for it. If she is holding hands with the guy and he catches you looking at his girl, the odds are that you have no chance.

If you happen to be seated right next to a girl you want to meet, make some light conversation and try to involve her even if she is with a guy. Make the conversation non-threatening and light. You will be able to tell if she likes her date or if she wants to talk to you. Don't, however, monopolize her conversation. After all, you are not taking her out. You will easily be able to figure out if she has some interest in you. Make sure, once again, that you remember her full name and place of work. In this situation, if you can't catch her on the way to the bathroom, be aggressive and ask the waiter to give her your business card when her date walks away. If she is interested, she will call. If not, at least you gave it a shot. Just remember to give the waiter a few bucks as incentive.

Bars are popular places to meet girls when you are in college and when you are in your twenties. Your social life during those years pretty much revolves around bars, and all guys have had great success in meeting girls in bars. In fact, the likelihood of spending the night with a girl you meet in a bar is greater than at any other place you meet a girl. This is because the girl is drunk, you are drunk, she is ready to play, she is trash, or some combination of the above. If you are just looking to get laid, go to a popular bar and roll the dice.

Large cities seem to have a tremendous turnover of popular bars, especially those that cater to people in their early twenties. The half-life of a new bar seems to be about six months to one year. The four-walls-and-a-bar theory comes to mind when discussing popular bars attracting people in their twenties. If you serve liquor and put a picture or two on the wall, you have a bar. In fact, if the pictures or decor even hint of some popular theme, you can have a catchy name and the masses will come.

When you get older, however, the only girls that hang out in bars are has-been or never-was-been, busted-up older ladies, who wear sleazy outfits, chain-smoke cigarettes, wonder why their voices are gravelly (years of cigarettes and alcohol), have skin like leather (too many unprotected suntans), and chase younger guys. The men wear ugly clothes, have chest hair coming out the top of their shirts, and wear too much jewelry and cologne. We have all seen them and all cities have bars that cater to them.

Streets and avenues are good places to meet ladies. You can meet dozens of people walking down the street every day of the week. You can meet people walking to and from work, during lunch hour, shopping, or just rollerblading on the street or in the park.

During the warm months in cities like New York, Chicago, and Atlanta, there are literally thousands of girls walking the streets during the day. There are dozens of great spots in every city to see very attractive women taking a stroll during lunch. In fact, if you take a half-hour walk during lunch during the spring or fall, you can't help but get a stiff neck from turning your head so often to look at the beautiful girls. It is enough to prevent you from going back to work in the afternoon.

Sports arenas have become a decent place to meet girls. If your local sports team is competitive, the sports arena is a very trendy place to be. Take a walk around the lower levels of the arena during a big game and you will see some very attractive ladies. Unfortunately, most of these girls are hanging on the arms of old, bald, and fat company executives with coast-to-coast (the comb-over haircut where the hair goes from one side to the other side) haircuts who just want to be seen with a trophy. Occasionally, however, there is some talent to harvest. Keep in mind, if she has talent, her friends will typically have talent too.

If you are lucky enough to meet an attractive girl at the arena, you are lucky in the fact that you know she is a sports fan. Most guys love sports and truly want to date a girl that at least has some interest in sports. Hopefully, however, she isn't a hockey or basketball groupie, only at the arena to meet an athlete.

The football stadium is not a great place to meet girls. A large majority of the fans at football games are of the male persuasion and when a talented female does appear, which is extremely rare, she is invariably at the game with a guy. Thus, it is not a great place to meet girls. It is, however, a great place to see a game.

Personal ads are for losers. I'm sorry, but this is very true. How can someone take out an ad for themselves? Basically, you are telling everybody that you have no life and can't meet anybody in any of the other places in this section. Perhaps these people should get out more often instead of sitting home and watching *Gossip Girl, Deadliest Catch,* or *American Idol.*

Have you ever seen some of these ads? Every girl advertised is beautiful and unique. Every guy is athletic and intelligent. If any of this shit was true, you wouldn't have to advertise this nonsense in a magazine because people would hit on you so often it would make your head spin. The following is a list of phrases frequently mentioned in personal ads. Please find *my* definitions of their meaning in the right hand column. I am sure you will agree.

Personal Ad Phrase	What the Phrases Really Mean
Single	Desperate
Female	Well, it isn't a man, so it must be a woman
Beautiful	Butt ugly
Intelligent	IQ greater than fifty
Unique	Bizarre
Athletic	Went to the gym this year
Tall	Above five feet tall
Different	Uncooperative
Sexy	Watches porno movies
Nice eyes	Ugly
Inner beauty	Extremely ugly
Bisexual	She says, "Sex?" I say, "Bye!"
Desperately seeking Susan	Susan is the only person who will go out with him
French man seeking woman	Considers himself French because he likes french fries
Professional	Has a job
Worldly	Can identify the U.S. on a map
Unconventional	Lives with his aunt
Divorced	Beat his wife
Sixtyish	Hasn't seen his sixties since the 1960s
Adventurous	Will be caught searching your apartment for valuables
Outdoorsman	Homeless
Timing	Owns a watch
Beautiful smile	Has all thirty-two teeth
Beautiful inside	Doesn't have a yeast infection

Avoid this area like the plague! Everybody claims to be a much better catch than they really are. You will be much better off going out with some friends and meeting some new people yourself.

Subways, trains, and buses are good places to meet girls. Thousands of people have met on mass transportation and have gotten married. In several cities, mass transportation is the predominant means of travel within the city, and since most people tend to be on the subway, train, or bus every day at the same time, it is relatively easy to meet someone you see three or four times a week.

The challenge develops when you are on the subway and see a girl whom you have never seen before, and realize that you have to meet her and get her phone number before either one of you gets off. The best way to do this is to throw caution to the wind and try to start a conversation. You have to get her business card before one of you gets to their respective stops. If not, you need to get her full name and place of employment so you can call her at the office. However, the safest way of showing interest is to give her your business card and tell her you would like to meet her for lunch on a specific day (offer two days). For example, "I would love to take you to lunch on Thursday or Friday, whichever works best for you." If she is interested, she will call you in the office. It is very non-threatening because it is a simple lunch and not a "date."

Your *apartment building* could be a great place to meet girls. You see the girls in the building all of the time and it is so easy to just say hello and introduce yourself. If you are too shy or haven't seen this person for a long time, make use of your doorman. You pay them a lot of money

Brad Berkowitz

on Christmas so make use of them. Ask your doorman to tell you a little bit about your desired lady. They may even be willing to introduce you to them or let them know that you are interested in meeting them.

Of course, dating someone in your building can present problems. During the first few months of the relationship, both of you are probably still dating other people. Should one or the other be caught taking another person back to their apartment, it will become an uncomfortable situation and could needlessly cause an end to the relationship.

In addition, if you break up with your girlfriend who lives in the building, seeing the girl so often can be very uncomfortable. Every time you bring another girl home, your ex will give her snide looks and the evil eye. Also, you will feel awkward when she brings her new boyfriend home and you see them together all of the time.

The *gym* is one of the best places to meet talent. It is so easy to casually walk over to a girl while she is working out at one of the machines and ask to work in with her. Conversation is natural and flows easily. In addition, if you know several people at the gym, it is easy to find somebody who knows her and will introduce you to her. If not, become friends with the personal trainers. They know everybody.

Another great reason why meeting people at the gym is beneficial is that you can see exactly what the girl looks like without makeup and without a lot of clothing. You see the real girl. If you like the girl when her hair is up and she is all sweaty, imagine what she looks like when she goes out. If, however, the girl works out with baggy pants and makeup, watch out. It only gets worse!

Work is the riskiest place to meet girls for several reasons. The first obvious reason is that it causes problems when you date somebody in your office. If things do work out, you really don't want anybody to know that the two of you are dating. This forces you to keep the whole relationship a secret. You sneak around the city when you go out and hope you do not run into anybody with whom you work. If you do, you will find yourself begging them not to tell anybody in the office. When too many people find out and you have asked them all to remain silent, you will find yourself owing favors to too many people.

If the relationship doesn't work out, the situation worsens. It is difficult to maintain a proper working relationship with this person and your coworkers will definitely notice the problem. The best case scenario in this situation is to not have both parties work in the same group any longer. You must fully focus on your career and try to avoid these types of distractions. You do not want to date somebody in the office and then have a belligerent breakup. It disturbs your work and that of your coworkers. There have been many cases where a hostile girl or guy will make life miserable for the other. Does *Disclosure* sound familiar?

A third reason why dating people in your office can present a problem is the question of promotions. Should one party have control over the promotability of the other, it causes ethical problems. You do not want anybody saying that your girlfriend is "sleeping her way to the top."

The strange thing about girls in the office is that you find yourself attracted to some of them once in a while. After all, you see these people all day and work with them very closely. Once in a while, you find yourself strangely attracted to them and once in a while, you also find yourself in bed with them. This is something most guys have done, and after doing it once or twice, they never would recommend it to any of their friends. While it could be very exciting to sleep with a girl with whom you work, the risk is not worth it.

Blind dates are bad. They are so bad that an entire chapter has been dedicated to this terrible thing. You will read that chapter coming up.

Vacations are great places to meet girls. You can meet girls from all over the world depending on where you go. The best part is that you are relaxed and looking to meet new girls. They are also looking to meet you, so go over to them and introduce yourself. The best vacations that guys have taken are those on which they have hooked up with some really attractive or exotic girls, or those where they met a really nice girl with whom they developed a meaningful relationship.

Most of your inhibitions go away when you are on vacation. When you are at home, most guys believe that they can date girls that are half their age plus seven (1/2 age + 7). This rule works very well if you think about it. A thirty-two-year-old can date girls that are at least twenty-three years old. When you were twenty-two, you could date girls that were eighteen and older. On vacations, however, most guys will change this rule a bit. The vacation formula becomes: 1/2 age + 3. Thus, at the age of thirty-two, you can date girls that are nineteen and older. Makes sense, doesn't it?!

Club Med, which typically should be covered under the vacations section, deserves its own section. If you can't hook up at Club Med, take out a personal ad because you are pathetic! This is the easiest place in the world to get some play. Girls that are as conservative as can be at home somehow become naughty girls at Club Med. Every activity they offer at Club Med is conducive to meeting girls. In fact, the GO's consider it their second most important priority to get you laid. (If you know the GO's at Club Med, you will know that the number one priority for them is to get themselves laid).

Club Med is highly recommended. It is a great place to have fun, relax, and meet people from all over the world. The weather is almost always terrific and the activities are fun. Just leave your inhibitions, not your rubbers, at home.

High-end department stores are fantastic places to meet girls. Go out of your way to walk through the perfume area at a store such as Bloomingdale's because the girls that work there are very attractive. It is relatively easy to meet one. Just walk over to the counter and tell her that you are looking to buy something for your mother. After a while, she will know that you are full of shit, but she won't care if she is interested. Try not to bother her for too long, however, because she is there to work, not get picked up. Be honest with her after a few minutes and tell her that you aren't there to buy perfume for your mother, but wanted to meet her. Her response will be the clue as to your next move.

Also, there are dozens of attractive women floating around the rest of the store on any given weekend. Don't take my word for it, go see for yourself. Just promise your friends that you will invite them to meet some of her coworkers.

Charity parties are terrific places to meet interesting people. Try to avoid those that are ten dollars or less. They don't attract much quality. The more expensive charity parties attract the best-looking ladies. Unfortunately, going to too many of these parties can exhaust your checkbook very quickly so try to find out which ones have had good parties in the past and attend those.

Many charity parties are black-tie. Guys really enjoy black-tie parties because all of the girls look great, and for some strange reason, they all seem to be nice (at least when they are at the party). Maybe it is because they look and feel great, or maybe it is because they feel they are helping a worthy cause. Whatever the case, many guys have had a great deal of success at these parties.

Apartment parties are also good places to meet people. The apartment is usually small enough that you can try to capture someone's attention rather easily. If you are uncomfortable approaching somebody by yourself, you should know at least a few people there that either know your desired girl or can at least introduce you to her. The major advantage of this type of party is that they are typically free to all comers. There is no entry fee and all the alcohol is usually free, unless it is BYOB. Apartment parties usually do not end too late, so you have the opportunity to ask your new friends to go out for some drinks in the neighborhood after the party.

Alcohol brand-sponsored events are informal cocktail parties given by promotional companies to push the particular brand name alcohol. Johnny Walker throws quality events throughout the country and they are always fun. They usually have eight to ten tables at the function, with each having its own bartender. The table is similar to a black-jack table and is loaded with Johnny Walker. If you like Scotch and like to meet new people, these events are for you. The alcohol and conversation flows like water, and the bartenders will make sure you have a good time.

A quality alcohol brand will usually be discreet in regards to the event and try to make the event as upscale as pos-sible. The quality of people that attend this event is high and you should be able to meet some nice people. The promotional company will also try to invite people that are older than twenty-five so that they can get a more mature crowd.

The *beach* is a wonderful place to meet girls. You can't hide anything at the beach so what you see is what you get. Avoid girls who wear big baggy clothes, eat big sand-wiches, and wear a lot of makeup. These girls have no self-respect and have never seen the inside of a gym, nor have they ever eaten a salad (with no dressing).

Guys like athletic girls and you can tell which girls are athletic at the outset. Guys like girls that will throw a football with them or play Kadima. Girls that lie around on the beach all day like a dead fish trying to get a tan bore most guys.

The beach is also a great place to meet people because, if you spot a girl you would like to meet, you can walk right up to her, or wait until she takes a walk and then casually get up off your butt and try to meet her. If you are somewhat shy about meeting someone new, there is usually somebody at the beach that knows her that would be more than happy to introduce you to her.

Skiing is a great place to meet girls. The actual skiing part of the day is not conducive to meeting girls, unless you ski like I do (crashing into people on the way down the mountain). The lodge at lunch and after skiing is a great place to meet people. Everybody seems open to meeting people at the lodge. The bar during happy hour is also a great place to meet people. Everybody wants to talk about their day skiing while relaxing by the fire. Set your target and move in for the kill.

Strip clubs seem to be getting more popular every day. However, many guys are not big fans of strip clubs because they would rather spend their money in pursuit of girls that will actually go out with them instead of pursuing girls who will only talk to them until their money runs out. Guys would rather have a naked girl in their bed at home than in their arms at a club, assuming she is hot of course. Plus, they don't need to spend that much money to get a girl naked in their bed.

We have all heard several stories of guys who have met strippers at these clubs and dated them thereafter, but how many of these relationships lasted (and how many of these guys got diseases)? I hope these guys remember to wear their "hats" when it is "raining" because with strippers, I would imagine that it rains hard and often.

Golf courses are not great places to meet girls. Unless you are at a country club, it is difficult to meet even an ugly girl at a golf course. Girls that are at the course tend to be playing with their boyfriends or husbands. Of course, a guy would love to meet a girl that belongs to a country club and plays golf. A perfect day for a guy would be if he could play golf in the morning and then hang out at the pool all afternoon with his wife. Dinner at eight o'clock, do the wild thing with your wife at night, and watch football all day Sunday. The perfect weekend!

Many of the girls you will meet at a golf course are usually described as "dikes on spikes," which is now a misnomer. I am sure that there are some very attractive girls somewhere that play golf, and you should continue to try to find them. In the meantime, play golf with your guy friends during the day and try to find girls at night.

Planes are great places to meet ladies. Think about it. If you are lucky enough to be seated next to an attractive girl on a plane, you can't avoid talking to her even if you wanted to! She is a prisoner of your conversation because she has nowhere else to go. She has to talk to you. If you make the conversation non-threatening and casual, you will have yourself a date. If not, you have yourself an uncomfortable plane ride.

Of course, I usually end up sitting next to the person that spills their food, the enormous person who drools on you while they sleep, or the person who holds their ever-crying baby.

College was a fantastic place to meet new girls. After exhausting the high school girls, guys are looking to have new experiences with new and exciting women from all over the country. Most guys lose their virginity in college, even though they will invariably lie and claim that they had sex all of the time in their parents' basement with their tenth grade girlfriend from high school.

The first few weeks in college can be like Mike Tyson at a beauty pageant. The freshman class is out to all hours of the night drinking in the local college bar. There is more scoring there than in a Florida Gators football game. After a while, the freshmen girls meet and date the older students, leaving the freshmen guys with the high school seniors from the local high school.

Movies are not great places to meet girls. The theater is dark, and even if you spot a fine looking girl in the theater, it is very difficult to meet her during the show. However, if you are a little lucky and spot her on the way out of the theater, you should try to ask her what she thought of the movie. Your window of opportunity is small so try to find out where she and her friends are going next and ask to join them.

However, if you spot one of your girl friends at the theater, go over and say hello. She may be with one of her attractive friends or going to a great party after the movie. Either way, it is in your best interest to find out.

Take a walk through *Saks* in Manhattan during the holiday season, starting from the entrance on Fifth Avenue at Forty-Ninth Street. Take thirty steps straight ahead and stop. Look around. It's like a beer commercial! The girls working there are beautiful and there are a lot of them. I don't know about the rest of the floors, but if you hang out on the first floor on the Forty-Ninth Street side, you will invariably see some of the best-looking women in New York.

South Beach, Miami, is a great place to meet girls. I know of several people that have brought girls back from South Beach and gotten married. There are more gorgeous models there than there are in any other place in the world. Stunning beauties, nice accommodations, laid-back attitudes during the day, and a wild nightlife. What else do you need (besides plane tickets)?! These girls are all looking to meet you because the guys that live down there are not interested in meeting them. For an explanation, refer to the movie *The Birdcage*.

The *Internet* is the latest way of meeting girls. I first got on the Internet at my friend's apartment when his wife was out of town. We wanted to see what this new thing was all about and immediately found ourselves logged into one of these dirty chat rooms. It really is amazing how some people get their kicks because we had hackers from all over the country offering to send us naked pictures of celebrities, friends, and even their wives. Though we didn't have the capability or desire to receive these pictures, we found out that we had been sent over three hundred pictures within ten minutes.

Other chat rooms allow you to converse with normal people from all over the country. We chatted with several ladies from three or four different states, and were invited to several parties in Charlotte, Charleston, and Orlando. My friend and I thought this new way of meeting people to be rather amusing at best.

Brad Berkowitz

Meeting people on the Internet (not including dating Web sites) is not one of the best places to find new people. It can be very dangerous and you never know what kind of people you will meet. I have met too many people that have claimed to have been excited to meet someone they had chatted with on the Internet, only to find them to be short, ugly, techno-nerds.

Meeting people on *dating Web sites* seems to work very well. People answer some simple questions, write some essays, post their pictures, and away they go. This method of meeting people works well because you are prospecting for dates even when you are doing other things. You can be at the gym, at work, on the subway, or even sleeping, and members of the opposite sex are reviewing your profile and sending you mail. This system works much better than blind dates because the person's picture is staring you right in the face. If you are not attracted to the person who sent you the message, simply send them a "no thank you" note. It is improper to disregard the letter; after all, the person thought enough about your profile to send you a note. The least you can do is send them a reply. However, if the person then replies with a mean response, you should simply block them and prevent them from contacting you again in the future.

There are, however, some things you need to be aware of when using these dating Web sites. First, many people use fake photos. Make sure that the person has more than one photo and both photos are of the same person. Second, many people tend to use old photos, some even taken as far back as college. Be aware that the person may not look like their photo when you meet them. If they don't, and you feel that the person misrepresented themselves, feel free to excuse yourself and leave. Third, people tend to describe themselves as athletic or in shape. Don't be surprised if these people have stretched the truth somewhat. Finally, be very aware of fake profiles. Many people in Ghana and Nigeria are stealing photos from people's profiles and creating phony profiles using these photos. You can recognize these profiles very easily. The photos are just too perfect, usually stolen from modeling Web sites. The English in the profile itself is very poor. The story these people tell you when you contact them is the same: they lost one parent in a car accident and they are tending to the other in Africa where they are in need of money. Don't fall for it! They are scams to have you wire money to them.

Meeting someone by *chance* is probably the way most people meet each other. You can't keep going to one or more of the above-mentioned places with your sole intention being to meet someone. You will meet someone when you least expect it and not when you are forcing yourself to go places to meet people.

IV. The Relationship

Guys can meet girls in just about every place imaginable. Whether you meet a girl in the subway, at the dry cleaner, a restaurant, or at a party, the thrill of meeting someone new is always exciting.

A typical guy will meet scores of girls, but not many special ones. When a guy meets somebody that intrigues him, nothing else around him exists. He totally focuses on this new girl and tries to isolate her in an area in which they can talk without any outside distractions. He wants the girl to know he is interested, and tries to find out if she is interested in him. If he can't isolate her or is pressed for time, such as in a subway, he tries to find out her full name, where she works, or some mutual friend whom he can contact to get the girl's phone number. On the occasions where he did not get the girl's number, a guy will frequent the bar, restaurant, or subway station until they see her again and get the digits.

THE FIRST DATE

After you get the digits, don't play games. If you don't call within three days, you are telling the girl you really aren't interested. Think about it. You made the effort to talk to the girl and ask for her phone number. Why wait to call her? If you don't want to date a girl that plays games, why play games with her?!

Your initial phone conversation will always go well. You seem to have so much in common at first and both of you are looking forward to the first date. The discussion leads to your plans for the weekend, and since both of you are so excited to see each other, both of you agree that it doesn't really matter where you go, as long as you get to spend time together and get to know each other. Boy, will things change in the future!

Since this is your first date and the conversation and chemistry are the most important things, don't go to an overly expensive restaurant. Sure, spending a lot of money on the first date will impress her, but where do you go from there? She may grow to expect it or, even worse, maybe there will not be a second date. You'll feel as if you wasted your time and money.

Make sure that your first date is not on a Thursday or Friday night. These are the best nights to go out with your friends and meet other girls. Until you've dated this girl a few times and you enjoy spending time with her, don't take her out on these two nights. Guys should start taking out girls on Thursday and Friday nights after they have been dating for a while.

What you wear is a big consideration. Unlike women, guys don't think all day about their attire for the evening. We just think about the place we are going to and dress appropriately. Girls, on the other hand, spend much more time deciding on their outfits. In fact, girls tend to spend more time dressing and undressing for their dates than Sally Struthers spends at the dinner table (no small accomplishment).

The conversation at the dinner table will determine everything. You could spill the wine, drop your napkin five times, or get food on your shirt, but still have a successful date as long as your conversation and chemistry are good. Try to avoid the conversation from becoming an interview. Yeah, sure, you want to get to know this person as well as possible, but if you shoot questions at her like a machine gun, she will become very defensive. Just relax and have fun.

When the date ends, walk her to the door. Whether she invites you in or not, if you are interested in seeing her again, let her know. Tell her that you had a good time and that you would like to see her again. Kiss her goodnight and go home. Of course, if you decide that you don't want to see her again, say good night and go to the local bar to take your chances with some of the leftovers at the bar! Make sure that if you don't want to see her again, you don't say something like, "I'll call you." Just say good night and walk away gracefully. Remember, always be a gentleman.

After the First Date

As you walk home from your first date, you are already deciding whether you want to see the girl again. If you decide that she isn't for you, *don't call*! We all have made this mistake several times and have only served to hurt somebody's feelings and prolong the inevitable. You are much better off forgetting about her and looking for another girl.

If you decide that you would like to see the girl again, call the next day! Tell her that you had a nice time and would like to see her again. Even if you can't schedule another date yet, call her. Tell her what you are thinking. Be honest, open, and direct. It will allow the relationship to progress in a similar fashion.

When you ask her out for the second date, you have passed "the interview." You know she is interested, at least you hope, and you feel more comfortable on the phone. Asking her out seems more relaxed and again you look forward to the next date.

Second Date

Both parties are more relaxed on the second date. After all, most relationships don't even get this far (most of Elizabeth Taylor's marriages don't even get this far).

Though the second date should be more fun than the first date, the interview process begins in earnest during this evening. You may begin to ask more risqué questions concerning past relationships, ex-partners, and even sex. Don't, however, divulge too much intimate information yet. There will be plenty of time to discuss these topics later in the relationship. Don't reveal your intimate secrets too early in the relationship. If the relationship doesn't last, you don't want to feel overly exposed to too many people in life.

The second date usually doesn't end with a goodnight kiss. The girl will invite you into her apartment for a drink or to watch television, but both of you know that the purpose is to fool around a little. Be very careful here. Don't press her to have sex. When the relationship progresses, you'll have more sex than you ever imagined. Don't worry, it will come sooner or later (and so will you).

Third Date

You have reached a third date and you obviously like the girl. (If you are going out with her just for the sex, give it up. You are better off with the Playboy channel and a tissue.) Now is where guys try to invoke the "Third Date Rule." Guys have some strange idea that they will have sex on the third date. (In fact, most guys believe this law to be as standard as getting dressed in the morning or the Detroit Lions losing each Sunday.) Why do guys think this way?! Doesn't the girl have any say in the matter? If you really like the girl, you should wait until both of you are ready. The sex and intimacy will be much better if you do. Besides, the rule doesn't always apply. We all have slept with girls on the first date and have also waited a long time to be with a girl. The only important thing is that both parties are ready.

A better way to judge when you will have sex with the girl for the first time is to find out if she has shaved her legs. Sound strange? Hardly! Several guys have been told by different girls that girls will shave their legs before the date when they want to have sex with their boyfriends for the first time. Of course, if it is summer, this theory may be more difficult to verify because girls tend to shave more often.

Regardless of what theory to which you subscribe, there are two rules you better follow when you have sex with a girl for the first time. You *must* spend the night and you *must* call her the next day. Girls are very particular about these two issues. They are much more emotional than guys and they don't want to feel that they have been used. Be a man. Stay over and call the next day to tell her how great it was. Guys tend to leave when they are done, and typically don't care about getting the girl off as well. Trust me, guys. Going down on a girl and getting her off is amazing. Don't just shoot your load and leave. If you can camp out down there and enjoy doing it, girls will go crazy. Try it!

THE INTRODUCTION

By now you may feel that the time is right to introduce your girlfriend to your friends. This is a big test because you value your friends' opinions. A guy should date a girl for over a month before he introduces her to his friends. Guys should not let too many people know whom they are dating. If you tell all of your friends and the relationship ends shortly, all of your friends will bombard you with questions about why you broke up. Instead, you should avoid all of the aggravation by only telling your friends about whom you are dating when you have been spending a lot of time with her.

When your friends meet your newest dating interest, their first opinion is crucial. Keep in mind that guys are extremely visual and very looks-oriented. It matters little to your friends if she is funny, smart, witty, caring, etc. It only matters if she is physically attractive. When your friends describe your date to their friends, they will say, "She's hot," "She's smokin'," "She's got a great body," or "She's nothing great." You can rest assured that the friends that meet your girlfriend are initially judging her on her appearance.

Assumptions

After about one month, a relationship will run into some challenging dilemmas:

1) *Are Saturday nights assumed to be your date nights?* This is usually the case. However, it really never seems to be discussed. Friday nights are typically the guys' night out (testosterone nights), and Saturday nights are date nights. At exactly what period in the relationship this occurs is a mystery to us.

2) *Is it assumed that you are to take your new dating interests to parties?* We don't know. Guys typically go to a lot of parties and there is no way we take a date to these parties at this stage in the relationship. However, I think it is safe to assume that you take your dating interest to parties where you know there will be other couples.

3) *Whom do you take to ballgames?* Guys are big sports fans and enjoy watching games with other guys. When we get tickets to a game, should we take a date, a friend, or a brother? The answer seems to be that you can take a date

to a regular season game, but playoff games or games with playoff implications are reserved for bigger sports fans.

4) *How many times do you see your girlfriend each week?* Difficult question. If you see her only once or twice a week, the relationship will not develop. If you see her four or five times per week, the relationship will develop quickly. I guess it depends on how you feel and if you are ready for the commitment.

5) *When you go out with your friends, are you supposed to invite your girlfriend?* Guys usually don't and it typically causes a problem. The girl will always ask if you are embarrassed to be seen with her or if your friends don't like her. You should do it once in a while, but not all the time, in order to keep all parties happy.

6) *When do you start taking her on business trips or company outings?* When you take a girl on a trip, you are instantly taking the relationship to another level. Whether you considered this girl your girlfriend or just a girl you are dating, you have just planted the seed in her head as well as in the heads of your colleagues that this girl is your girlfriend. If you don't take her on a company trip, you may find yourself one lonely man in a small town. You may even come home to your hotel late at night after a few shots of Johnny Black and call your girlfriend to ask, "So, what are you wearing?"

Family Introduction

I have always had a problem with this. My parents would invite me to dinner, the beach, a party, a show, etc., and

ask me to bring a date. I have always felt that if I introduce a girl to my parents, and especially grandparents,
that all parties will consider her to be my girlfriend. The
parents will harass me for weeks asking how she is. My
grandmother will tell her friends at the bridge club that I
was getting married and she will start going through the
mothballs in the closet looking for the right dress for the
wedding. (Trust me. The right dress always seems to be
the same one she wore at the last five family weddings.)
Most importantly, the "girlfriend" now thinks I am in
love with her. After all, she met the parents and they
approve. One time after a girlfriend met my parents for
the first time, she asked me what kind of china patterns I
wanted to have in *our house*!

The Critical Month

When a relationship enters the third month, the situation
becomes more complicated. You have been dating for a
while and both of you start thinking about where the relationship goes from here. You are beyond the stage where
you wonder if you see each other every Saturday, and now
you have to decide how many times during the week you
will see each other. One person may tell the other that he/
she would like to see the other more often and, unless the
other person agrees, the relationship could die right there.
It is over. If you want to step up the pace and your partner
doesn't, you've basically been told that this relationship
isn't going anywhere. Should this happen, you have to
realize that this relationship isn't going the distance and
it is time to cut your losses.

When both parties want to proceed, you are now boyfriend and girlfriend. Get used to it guys because if you don't introduce her as your girlfriend, you will hear it from her. After all, she probably has considered you her boyfriend from the first time you slept with her. Don't offend her by referring to her as your friend. In fact, if you don't use the phrase, "this is my girlfriend, _____," she will be very angry because she always introduces you as, "this is my boyfriend, _____."

ENGAGEMENT AND MARRIAGE

Never been there! Never done this! Never even been close! Consult another book for more information on this topic.

BREAKUP

Neil Sedaka said it best, "Breaking up is hard to do." Whether you are breaking up with her or she is breaking up with you, it hurts. Guys are not good at breaking off relationships, but we have learned through the years that it is best to address it quickly and get it over with. Don't prolong it and don't get into a three-hour discussion about it. You don't want to be too abrupt, but the other party is probably expecting the termination anyway, so get on with it. Explain how you feel and that you believe that the two of you are not right for each other long-term. Have compassion and tell her that it is for the best. Wish her well and move on. Never breakup by e-mail, voicemail, or Facebook status updates.

It is not as easy when she breaks up with you. We all have been hurt in relationships by girls for whom we cared much about. But just as in the case when you break up with her, you should be able to see it coming

The best way to cope with your loss is to go out with your friends. God knows that they have sought your advice several times over the years. You have always been there for them so seek them out. Good friends will help you through the pain. Everybody has been hurt in relationships before, so your friends can empathize with you. Don't sit in your apartment and watch depressing movies because you'll rot. Don't wait for her to call because she won't (and you should not call her). Go out and meet new people. Meeting a girl on the rebound is not the best way to meet somebody and form a new relationship, but ending up in the arms of a new woman doesn't suck!

V. Blind Dates

Blind dates are predominantly a big waste of time. Everybody feels the need to set guys up with somebody that *they* think is right for us. People always say they know somebody perfect for us, but it rarely even leads to a second date, let alone a relationship. If you can think of all of the blind dates you have had, and all of the time, effort, and money you have wasted, why do you continue to go on them?

The whole process of blind dating is awkward. Somebody you know gives you a girl's phone number and asks you to call her. You don't want to call this new girl the first two days because it makes the girl think you are desperate. By the third day, when your friend calls and asks why you have not yet called his/her friend, you promise to call that night.

The initial call is like an interview. What do you ask somebody you don't know and aren't sure you want to meet anyway? "Where are you from?" "How old are you?" "Where did you go to school?" "What do you do?" "Do you know …?" (the stereotypical Jewish geographical question) These are all the typical icebreakers that lead into superficial conversation about nothing. Honestly, the only thing a guy really wants to know is if the girl he is supposed to meet is hot. (Just one time, I'd like to ask, "So, which supermodel do you most resemble?") Yes, I will admit it, guys are very looks conscious. If she isn't attractive, the date is pointless, and we hope she feels the same. Guys will rarely get into a relationship with someone if we are not physically attracted to them.

The initial conversation really should only last fifteen minutes, but invariably we end up speaking for about an hour. The last forty-five minutes of conversation should really be avoided because you do not even know this person yet. There is ample time on the date and in subsequent phone conversations to get to know this person. Extending an initial phone conversation only raises your expectation level, and you set yourself up for the inevitable disappointment. In addition, you will feel as if you have wasted your time if the date is bad, so keep the conversation brief.

Sometimes, however, the last forty-five minutes can be very entertaining. I remember that a friend of mine set me up with a girl she met once. I was skeptical at first, but called that week. She seemed very nice and after the initial fifteen minutes of interview questions, she changed the topic of conversation to sex. She initiated it by stating that she didn't sleep around and that she had not had sex in eighteen months. I told her that if that had been my situation, I would have had such a severe case of MSB (massive sperm buildup) that sperm would be shooting out of my ears. When asked how she could abstain for so long without sex, she told me, during our first-ever conversation I must reiterate, that she had sex toys she used to satisfy herself. Needless to say that I changed all of my plans that week to meet her!

When you finally decide to end the initial conversation, you have to make a date. After all, that's why you called. It does not matter that you may have had a terrible conversation; you are forced to make plans. Hopefully, you were smart enough not to make dinner plans! Never take a blind date to dinner! When you take a blind date to dinner, you have forced yourself into a dollar and time commitment with somebody you do not know, and probably will not ask out again. All guys learn the hard way that the best thing to do is to meet for a harmless drink or coffee after work, and put a strict time limit on the date. Forty-five minutes! This way, you meet casually and get to know each other in non-threatening or non-expensive surroundings.

Do not plan to spend more time together than you originally planned! Even if you really like the girl, you are better off ending the date early. She may not feel the same way about you and you would only be wasting your time. If she does like you, she will be excited to hear from you when you call her the next day.

Now that the time arrives and you are in the elevator of her building about to pick her up for the first time, several thoughts are going through your mind: Will I find her attractive? Will her cat's litter box smell rancid? Would I rather date her stunning roommate? What streets should we walk on if she isn't attractive? Will I run into anybody I know while on the date? Did I remember to trim my nose hairs? Will I finally see that girl I met at the gym and have wanted to meet for six months while on this stupid waste-of-time date?

You ring the bell and she opens the door. Boom! The first visual. Is it her or her roommate? It is her and she looks nothing like what your friend said? Courtney Cox?! I don't think so. More like Wally Cox! What do you do now? You can't say that you are a Domino's delivery man because you are not wearing an orange and blue shirt and a bicycle hat. You introduce yourself, walk in, compliment her apartment, and thank the big man in heaven that you remembered to put a time limit on this date. If you didn't remember the time limit and were foolish enough to agree to meet for dinner, you start wondering if you can write the date off on your taxes as a bad date expense.

So, off you go on your blind date. You wonder why they call these blind dates. Is it because your friend must have been blind to have set you up with such a beast, or is it because even Stevie Wonder would not find this girl attractive? You are not attracted to her at all and wish that the two of you had made an agreement stating that if one or both of you weren't attracted to the other, he/she/both could say so up front and the date would be canceled. In a perfect world, all blind dates would begin that way (and in a perfect world I would be dating Ali Landry). Guys would not have a problem at all if their date told them not to proceed when they walked into her apartment. Yeah, sure, it would be a blow to your ego at first, but you would rather know up front and not waste your time and money by going out with a girl that did not like you.

Guys know within five seconds if they want to proceed with the date. If we are not physically attracted to her, we would rather go home and do laundry. The date is point-less. But, no, this type of agreement doesn't exist in the real world, so we have to go out with this girl.

You leave her apartment and walk to the restaurant. You planned out the route you take to walk because you do not want to run into somebody you know. Should you encounter a friend while on a blind date, try to avoid introducing the girl as your blind date.

The choice of restaurants is an interesting topic, assum-ing you didn't listen to my previous advice. You do not want to go to an expensive restaurant and spend money on a girl you do not plan on ever seeing again. You also do not want to go to White Castle, unless of course you tell her that you are taking her to that fancy new French restaurant called Le Chateau Blanc. You can also make reservations at two restaurants and use one of them de-pending upon whether you like the girl or not (remember to cancel the second reservation).

The conversation at dinner can go one of two ways. You can hit it off, at least socially, and the date can be enjoy-able, or you can totally clash in which case you would rather go home and watch the paint peel off the walls. Either way, you begin thinking about ways to end the date. My sister-in-law told me a story once of a guy who took her out on a blind date and asked his friend to beep him halfway through the date. If he did not like his date, he would gracefully tell her that it was urgent and would have to leave immediately. Needless to say, that the gentle-man in question remained with my beautiful sister-in-law on the date, but she read right through the scheme and blew him off and went on to meet a much better guy, my brother.

I have had some interesting things happen during a blind date. One date got so drunk during dinner that she stood up, walked over to me, sat on my lap, and started kissing me in the middle of the restaurant. Although not a major problem, I am not one to fool around with somebody in the middle of a busy restaurant. However, when she passed out on my lap and proceeded to throw up her eight Cuervo shots on my shoulder, it became a problem.

Anyway, you have now completed dinner and you ask the waiter for the damage. You are so anxious to leave that you give the waiter your credit card just as he gives you the check. Try to avoid doing that. You are only telling the girl how badly you want to leave. Try to be patient and wait at least five minutes before paying the check. Help your date with her coat and leave.

You continue to scout the streets for people you know as you walk your date home. She suggests going for a drink, but you'd rather go home and catch an old episode of *Mr. Ed* or *Frasier* than continue the date. After what seems like two hours, you arrive at your date's apartment and she invites you inside. There are about a dozen reasons why you would rather not go inside, but the only one that comes to mind is that she is butt ugly, so you just say that you are tired and want to go home. Panic immediately strikes. The most awkward part of the evening has arrived. How do you say good-bye? You don't want to offend her, but at the same time, there is no way in hell you want to see her again. Do you shake hands or kiss her good night, and if so, where? Try this. Just say good night, kiss her on the cheek, and leave. Never say, "I'll call you." Then remind yourself never to go on another blind date again, even though you know that you will do this drill all over again next month.

Stupidly, most guys do not let it end there. Some guys have a very bad habit of calling girls periodically, but not asking them out. Why?! I don't know. I guess guys just feel bad about not calling after getting to know someone. Do not do this because it only prolongs the agony.

So, what have we learned about blind dates? A lot, and nothing at all. There are a bunch of rules you should follow should you foolishly decide to go on a blind date. You should follow these rules strictly, even though we have all broken every one of them and will continue to break them:

1. *Never agree to date a girl that is recommended to you by your grandmother.* Their tastes in girls is pathetic. The worst! Grandmothers just want to introduce you to the granddaughters of their bridge club partners. My grandmother once tried to set me up with a girl who could have been an Eastern European Olympic weightlifter. She might have been able to give Mike Tyson a run for his money.

2. *When one of your girl friends wants to introduce you to one of her friends, get a guy's opinion first.* Girls always think that all of their friends are gorgeous. Guys will give you a more accurate description. Since guys want to date girls that are attractive, wouldn't it make more sense to get another guy's opinion? Save yourself the

problem of going out with a girl who may not suit your taste and get a guy's opinion.

3. *When you ask the introducer if the girl is attractive and he/she says that the girl is nice, funny, or has nice eyes, you are in big trouble.* If the girl in question is attractive, the introducer would answer affirmatively immediately. Any delay means *no*! Your time is too valuable to waste. You know that if the girl in question is not physically attractive, you will not want to see her again. Thus, you are saving both of you the time and effort.

4. *Never go on a blind date on Thursdays, Fridays, or Saturdays.* These are the best nights of the week to go out with your friends and meet girls that you like, not nights to spend time with somebody that your friend thinks you will like. These three nights are the best nights to go out, so take advantage of your opportunity. Go out, have fun, and meet new people. Go on your bad blind date on a Monday, Tuesday, or Wednesday.

5. *Be wary of someone who has several friends he/she would like you to meet.* If the introducer really thinks they know who your match is, then how come they have five friends that are good for you?! Ideally, you would think that someone introducing you to a girl would have that one special person in mind. If they have several, you should ask the introducer if you could get a group of guys and girls together and all go out one night. This way you could meet them all in one night and ask out the one you like, if any.

6. *Never introduce your blind date as your blind date.* It is rude and will ruin the rest of your evening. You are already not interested, why make the situation worse? The girl will be offended because what you are really telling her and your friend is that if you weren't out with her on a blind date, you wouldn't even be seen in the same county as her.

7. *Do not take a blind date to dinner.* You do not know this person and do not want to spend money on somebody in whom you have no interest. Even if you do like her, she may not like you. Be smart. Go for a drink. It is less costly, more efficient, and you can put a time limit on it.

8. *If you break Rule 7 and do go to dinner, go to a moderately-priced, casual restaurant.* Expensive and romantic restaurants are inappropriate. Go to a casual, inexpensive restaurant that will allow the two of you to talk. Get to know her first before you take her to a nice restaurant. You will be wasting your time if you take her to a fancy restaurant and then you never see her again.

9. *Put a time limit on the duration of the date.* There is plenty of time to spend together later on if both of you are interested in each other. You probably will not like her anyway, so you will be saving yourself some time.

10. *Be mature.* You agreed to go on this date, so try to enjoy the conversation. Girls are fully aware that guys will have their friends page them during dinner. Try to get to know her as a person. Maybe she really isn't

that bad a person after all. If she likes you, but isn't interested in you romantically, she might be willing to introduce you to some of her attractive friends. Also, you are likely to run into her again in the future, so be pleasant.

11. *Walk the girl home promptly to her door.* Tell her it was nice to meet her. If you are not interested, which you will not be, don't kiss her or say you will call her. Just say good night and leave. Then go home, call the introducer, and rip him/her another asshole for thinking that you would like this person in the first place.

12. *Do not call the girl if you are not interested in dating her.* I did this on several occasions hoping to remain friends, but it only led the girl to believe I was interested. There is no reason at all to call her again. You did not like her so why waste both your time and her time. Move on and go meet girls by yourself.

13. *Yes, it is ok to go on two blind dates in one night.* I know that sounds horrible, but look at it this way: blind dates are like interviews anyway, and since you can do two interviews in one day, why not do two blind dates. I would choose a quiet night, like Monday. I would go to the gym after work to get relaxed. I would typically meet the first girl around 7:00 or 7:30 PM for a drink. The second I would meet around 8:30 PM or so. You have to make sure you don't drink too much on either date, and give yourself enough time in between dates to relax and to get to the second bar. Never make the two dates at the same bar; you are bound to get caught. You will look bad even though you are doing absolutely nothing wrong.

VI. Why Guys Do the Things They Do

Girls and guys are always discussing and analyzing why members of the opposite sex do the things they do. The following seem to be the most asked questions concerning guys and girls. In this section, I will answer all of the most asked questions about the ways guys think, and then attempt to answer some of the things guys want to know about women.

Why do men say they are going to call and then never do? There are several ancillary reasons why guys do not call, but the basic reason is that they are just not that interested. Girls have to consider where they met the guy in the first place. If they met in a bar, the answer is obvious. Most guys will say or do just about anything to get a girl to like him. Men are led by their penis, while women are led by their heart. When a guy has a drink, every girl begins to look better. A plain-looking girl suddenly becomes attractive to a guy after a few drinks. Each beer raises a girl's rating by half a point (and each Scotch will raise a girl's rating one point). For example, if a guy thinks that a girl is a five at best, five beers or two to three Scotches will make her look like a ten. Even Phyllis Diller becomes a ten by the eighth or ninth Scotch.

If a girl meets a guy somewhere else and the guy takes the number but doesn't call, he is just not interested at all. Sometimes a guy will feel obligated to take a number if he has been talking to a girl for a long period of time. Sometimes a guy is not sure if he is interested, so he will take the number and call if he has nothing else to do. Perhaps he has a girlfriend and wants to put the girl into his inventory should he and his current flame split.

Finally, a guy may take a girl's number during their conversation hoping that he may get some play that night. The seven digits act as a false sense of security that the guy will call her even if they fool around that evening. This is a scam that many guys use to get some action during the same night. Depending on whether they get some that night, they will or will not call the girl at all. Usually, a guy will call her again only if they had some wild, hot relations that same night.

Why do men want to leave after having sex? A woman has a more level sex drive during the act than a man. A guy is interested in sex as long as the woman can keep him hard. Once he comes, his sex drive is nil. He would rather go home and watch the Mets lose one in the ninth inning than stay at the girl's apartment after sex. A guy feels power in bed when he is hard, but once he comes, he feels vulnerable, whether the feeling is conscious or not. A girl should understand this and realize that when a guy does stay over, he really likes her. Guys would rather have sex and then sleep alone in their own bed, while girls want to cuddle all night. In addition, a guy doesn't like to be touched down there right after sex. A girl should leave it alone for some time until it feels strong enough again to rise to the occasion.

When a guy leaves, under most situations he doesn't really like the girl. He just wants the sex and then wants to go home. He doesn't give a shit about her feelings and is probably just using her. If a guy really likes the girl, he will spend the night and even do it again in the morning. Remember that sex is more physical for a guy and more emotional for a woman, especially when the two haven't known each other too long.

Why do men cheat in relationships? The male animal is not naturally monogamous. If you look at any other animal, the male will have a bunch of women in his herd, pride, etc. Male lions will maintain as many as eight lionesses and have been known to have sex with them as many as forty times a day (that's what I call a king of the beasts). Though, even at that rate, a male lion will not surpass the sexual prowess of Wilt Chamberlin; it still is a pretty impressive number. Women have to realize that men give love to get sex, while women give sex to get love. Sex is a much more emotional thing for women than it is for men. A man could have sex with another woman while dating his girlfriend and walk away from the encounter without feeling regret. All he feels is the great orgasm he had with her. Women on the other hand usually feel a much bigger emotional bond with their lovers. Sex is a much more intimate event for them.

Men will cheat for several reasons. Most of the time when men cheat, it is to get a quick release. They are attracted to the new woman and only want to have sex with her to feel good. There is absolutely no emotional attachment whatsoever. They may also cheat because their current sex life has been boring, or because they are feeling that they might no longer be attractive to other members of the opposite sex. They have sex with a new woman to make themselves feel better mentally and emotionally.

In addition, most cultures in the world are not truly monogamous. Monogamy is actually the exception rather than the norm throughout the world. Most of the cultures throughout Africa and the Middle East actually encourage men to take multiple wives.

Why do women cheat? Most of the time, women cheat because they feel neglected by the men in their lives. Sex is more of an emotional thing for a woman, so it is more difficult for her to cheat if all other things in her current relationship are good. A woman will rarely cheat if she is emotionally satisfied with her current relationship.

Why is it that guys have to call women and have to ask them out? Guys, by nature, like to pursue women. Thus, they feel that they have to call the woman first and ask her out first. However, this situation is changing. Many women now feel confident enough to pursue men. They have to be careful, however, because an overly aggressive woman will be assumed to be a little loose sexually. Besides, I do not know of too many guys that have been pursued by really attractive girls. The girls that pursue guys are usually not the girls that the guy would be interested in anyway. If he felt that she was attractive, his opinion is that he would already have approached her. The only case I know where an attractive girl pursued a guy was when Halle Berry went to extremes to meet David Justice, then of the Atlanta Braves. Outside of that, most girls that approach or ask out guys are not the girls that we want to meet.

Though guys are flattered when a girl calls him to ask him out, there is really a better way that a girl should approach it. She should let him know that she is interested in him without pursuing him. Some guys get a little defensive when pursued by girls. The girl should ask one of their mutual friends or acquaintances to introduce them or let him know that she asked about him. If the guy is interested, he will call.

Why is it that we only meet attractive people of the opposite sex when we are dating somebody else? People will invariably meet the most attractive people of the opposite sex when they are either on a date with someone or dating somebody. When people are single, they tend to meet quantity and not quality. In addition, when somebody meets one interesting person, they will invariably meet several others within a short period of time. Rarely will you only meet one intriguing person at a time. Perhaps it's confidence, or an I-don't-care attitude.

Why does every girl say that looks aren't important? My first question to these girls is, "If you saw two guys at a bar and you were going to approach one of them, which would it be?" Of course there are countless other things that are important, but physical attraction is a very good starting point. When I ask married girls if they would have married their husbands if they didn't find him good looking, they invariably say, "That's different." My answer is, "How is it different?!"

Girls are hung up on the fact that guys are extremely visual when it comes to being attracted to girls. However, girls are just as visual, though they will never admit it. Girls are always talking to each other saying how cute a particular guy is or how handsome he is. They never seem to say how smart or generous he is. Guys, don't let girls fool us. They are looking for visually attractive members of the opposite sex as much as we are.

Do guys notice your perfume? You bet we do! All guys have favorite perfumes and will definitely notice it. A girl's perfume, if worn in subtle amounts, could be a huge aphrodisiac. Guys should be aware of the perfumes that work for them and know their names. Girls like it when you know and compliment their perfume.

Bad perfume, on the other hand, is a big buzzkill. A beautiful woman will instantly become less desirable when her perfume is rancid. In addition, when a girl wears too much perfume it is a big turnoff. Guys don't want to be able to smell their dates from across the street. Perfume should be flattering and subtle, and should have the effect that the girl wants—to attract her date.

Do guys notice jewelry? Absolutely, as long as it is not overly done and it doesn't include nose rings. Nose rings look terrible. It looks primitive and disgusting. And what happens if you have to blow your nose? Would snot come shooting out the side of the nose? I guess it would make having a cold even more uncomfortable.

Why do guys like to read in the bathroom? What else are you supposed to do in there? Guys like to do two things at once, and it is a great place to relax and read the paper.

You can get some of your best reading done in the stall. It is also important to allow your guy friends the same opportunity by leaving the sports section in the bathroom. My question to girls should be why they *don't* read in the bathroom. It is almost as instinctive for guys as the act itself.

Why do guys not think that girls' friends are gorgeous? Every girl thinks that her friends are all gorgeous. I can't believe what some girls think is gorgeous! A guy should always get another guy's opinion before being introduced to a girl by one of her friends. Girls just do not know what guys like in girls. Similarly, guys don't know what girls look for in guys, so they don't know which of their friends are good looking.

Why don't guys want to kiss girls after they smoke cigarettes? Because guys think that smoking cigarettes is the single most disgusting habit. I only dated one girl in my life that smoked and I finally got her to quit (we ironically broke up one month later). I also got my parents to quit smoking (no, I never kissed them, lol). Kissing girls that smoke is really not enjoyable. Shock therapy works well on girls that continue to smoke, and I hear it is going to be legal in the United States by the end of the year.

Why do guys like to quote television shows and movies? Wouldn't it be nice to date a girl that would know what you are talking about when you say, "Don't be saucy with me, Bernaise!", "One must go to a bowling alley to meet a woman of your stature," or "Looking good Louis, feeling good Todd"? Guys like to test each other with quotes from television shows or movies, so get used to it girls.

Why will a guy ask out a girl for a second date if he really isn't interested? Maybe the guy is trying to get sex, but that is just about the only thing I have come across. You didn't have a good time on the first date, why go on a second? As if it is going to get better? You didn't like this person the first time when they were supposedly on their best behavior, so how can you like them when they stop putting up that nice front? Don't waste your time.

Why do all guys want to be with two women at the same time? Why not?! It is every guy's ultimate fantasy. There are three types of guys in this world: 1) those that want to be with two girls at once and freely admit it; 2) those that want to be with two girls at once, but lie and say they don't; and 3) gay guys. The female body is beautiful and men find it sexually stimulating to be involved with more than one girl at once. Maybe it is a power thing or just a sexual thing. However, we all want to do it.

Why don't girls know what they are looking for when they go shopping? When a guy goes shopping it is because he needs something. When a guy needs a pair of slacks, he goes to the store and looks for a pair of slacks. Women, on the other hand, go into gathering mode when they go shopping. They love to just wander around aimlessly with no destination in mind. They can spend hours just walking around the malls or shopping centers with nothing in particular in mind. Guys go to the store, get what they want, and go home.

The only thing guys like to gather when they go shopping is girls. They love to check out the salesgirls and any girls that happen to be shopping in the same store as them. A guy will even ask to be helped by the most attractive girl in the department, whether she works at the store or not.

Why did God only make women multi-orgasmic? How come God allowed women the enjoyment of coming several times within a few minutes? Women are like machine guns. They can shoot their load rapid fire. Men are like muskets. It takes us a long time to reload. Imagine if we were able to be a machine gun for just one day! Human males got a raw deal.

Why do women grow more hair when they get older and guys lose their hair? Women start getting hair growing out of their faces and guys start losing hair off their heads. I guess God tried to at least pay guys back for hair loss by giving us the ability to grow hair out of our noses and ears. Great trade!

Why do guys want to date girls that are sports fans? Guys are usually very interested in sports and would like to share their interests with their girlfriends. Just once I want to take a girl to the Meadowlands and, after Eli Manning throws a touchdown pass, I want her to point out to me how Manning looked off the safety. What a turn-on that would be!

Why are girls always late? Every girl that I have ever dated has always been late. They are never on time. I don't think they understand the concept of time. Granted, I know it takes them a lot longer to get ready to go out, but wouldn't you think that they would compensate for that? Why do I always have to wait for my date or girlfriend at the time to finish getting ready?

Obviously, to get around this problem, guys have to compensate for them. Always tell your date to be ready fifteen minutes before you would actually want her to be ready. This way, you will not mind waiting the fifteen minutes while she finishes, because you will not be late.

Why do girls change their moods on a daily basis? Every girl I have ever known changes her moods daily, some more so than others. I think it makes the relationship more exciting because it seems that you are really dating several girls because you don't know which one will show up.

I guess the reason would be because girls' hormonal levels are different every day. Think about what would happen to guys if their testosterone levels changed every day. On some days we would have the urge to have sex with every girl in the office, while other days we would not want anybody to touch us because our nipples hurt.

Why do girls always plan their outfits a long time in advance? What a woman wears is very important to them. They can't be seen in the same outfit twice or they think they will be the object of other girls' comments all evening. Once you make plans with a woman for a specific evening or they receive an invitation to a party or wedding, they forget about everything else that is important to them at the time, and immediately start thinking about what outfit they will wear to the event. In fact, most girls will even call several of their friends for advice as soon as they have plans. What is funny about that conversation is that the friend will know the girl's entire wardrobe and give advice to the girl without ever getting suggestions! It's amazing. Imagine a guy calling another guy and asking him if he should wear his blue suit or his gray suit. The friend would think he is a jerk for bothering him and hang up.

A girl is also very conscious about what other girls are wearing. Go to a party and look at what the girls are wearing. All of the girls will be wearing the newest fashions. Every girl at an event will check each other out and know exactly what they are wearing. If you happen to take a girl to a wedding or party, I guarantee you that if you ask her at the end of the night what she thought of a specific girl's outfit, she will know exactly what she was wearing.

Imagine what happens when two girls at the office or at a party are wearing the same dress or outfit. They will feel humiliated and feel very uncomfortable. They spent a lot of time and effort in shopping for this outfit and picking it out of their closet. Now they see another girl wearing the same outfit. Trust me, you haven't seen two girls really avoid each other and feel uncomfortable until you run into this situation. Neither one may ever wear that outfit again.

Anyway, it's what the guy wears that determines how formal/informal the girl looks at the event. You may think that to be very chauvinistic but read on and I am sure you will agree. Picture a girl at a party and she is wearing a dress. If her date is wearing a short-sleeved polo shirt, shorts, and sneakers, she will look very casual. Now, if the same girl wears the same dress, but her date is wearing a blazer, slacks, and shoes, she looks more formal. It may sound foolish, but give it a try some time.

Why do old ladies wear hairnets? I mean, they already wear that disgusting smelling hair spray. Wearing a hairnet and hair spray at the same time is similar to wearing contact lenses and eyeglasses at the same time.

What age women should a guy date? Most guys like to date younger women. They look better, have more energy, and look up to us. An older woman is fun to date when you are in your teens and early twenties because it makes you feel more mature, and you think that it impresses your friends. However, as a guy approaches his thirties, he should not date older women. Older women want to get serious a lot quicker and promote marriage. Their biological clocks are running and they want you to catch them. Besides, men in their thirties tend to age more gracefully than do women of the same age. Be smart, guys, date younger women. The relationship will progress at your speed and you will be a lot more relaxed.

Should a guy ever ask a woman her age? Are you kidding? Absolutely! Maybe not in the first few minutes, but if you intend on dating this girl, don't you want to know how old she is? The only girl that will not tell you her age is the type that is trying to hide something. Remember, age is just a number. However, if you adhere to the logic that you will not date a girl older than you, you better find out how old the girl is before the relationship proceeds.

Not only do you need to know her age, you better find out how much baggage she brings to the table. Has she ever been married before? Is she still in love with her ex-boyfriend? Does she have any children, and if so, are they legitimate? You have to avoid girls that have excessive baggage because you will be inheriting all of it. You should try to enter into a new relationship with as little baggage as possible. She wants to know your baggage so make sure you know all of hers.

Is money a big issue? Ideally, it really shouldn't be. If two people love each other, money should not be a big issue. Realistically, however, money does play a major role in the success of relationships. Many guys are intimidated by girls that outearn them. Guys tend to think that they should be the principal breadwinner in the family, and that any income that the girl contributes is icing on the cake. Nowadays, many girls outearn their husbands or boyfriends and unless the guy is secure enough with this situation, it will cause problems.

Money can also be a problem when one party, usually the guy, is in school and not earning money, or is just starting a new business. Some girls don't understand that guys in these stages of their careers need to be extremely careful in regard of the amount of money that they spend. If a girl isn't willing to wait for him to start his career or graduate school, she isn't worth her salt. You are better off to get rid of her now than wait for her to blow you off for that spoiled brat driving daddy's BMW.

Another result of a woman having more money than a guy is that she could control him, especially if that money is her father's money. If a girl is going to use her money to control the guy, you will develop a "honeydew relationship," honey do this and honey do that. Unless the girl doesn't hold the money issue over the guy's head, the relationship is doomed and the guy will be miserable. Remember as an example, Daniel Stern's character and his wife in *City Slickers*.

Will guys shy away from women who have been with too many other guys? Absolutely, and, of course, this is a double standard. A guy wants to be with women that have been around or are easy, but when it comes to having a serious relationship, he won't give that girl the time of day. Guys don't want to have a serious relationship with sleazy girls. When guys decide that they finally want to settle down and meet Ms. Right as opposed to Ms. Right Now, he will change his social habits. Now, he will frequent fewer bars and will look for a different type of woman. Values, family, personality, intelligence, and a feeling that she would make a good mother become much more important than plastic breasts, drop-dead looks, and great sex (well, most of the time).

In addition, when a woman has a reputation that precedes her regarding the amount of men she has satisfied, fewer men, given the amount of diseases that can be sexually transmitted, will find her attractive. Back in the sixties, seventies, and early eighties, guys would actually pursue these types of girls. Nowadays, however, guys are much more careful about whom they bed.

What do guys like in bed? Guys hate monotony. They love spice and change. You have to keep the sex interesting or the relationship will fail. Experiment with new things. Guys, contrary to popular belief, really enjoy making girls come. There is nothing like the feeling knowing that you have just made a girl feel as good physically as she possibly can.

Guys also do enjoy it when girls initiate sex. Don't get into a routine whereby the guy always has to start the sex act. Girls don't realize how powerful they could be if they called their boyfriends during the day and just told them that they couldn't wait to get home that night so they could have sex. Trust me; a guy won't be able to concentrate on anything else the rest of the day.

Guys also like to take their time when having sex with women. Women are correct in this sense. If a guy wants to get her naked in one minute and sleep with her in the second minute, he really doesn't like her as much as he claims. When a guy really wants to be with a woman, he enjoys staring into her eyes, kissing her passionately, and making the whole process last. Guys and girls should communicate both physically and verbally to fully enjoy the act. Both parties should tell each other how they feel and what they like and don't like about sex. Communication is the most important part of the process.

How long must a woman keep a man waiting before having sex with him? While there is no direct correlation between the amount of time you wait before having sex for the first time and whether the relationship will last, it probably is a good idea to wait at least a few dates for several reasons. Firstly, you will show her that you really care about her and that you are not seeing her only for the sex. It will make her feel more comfortable. Secondly, if you have sex very early in a relationship and you break up with her shortly thereafter, you will make her feel cheap and used. You are much better in the long run (of course not in the short run) not to have slept with her at all. Her feelings will be spared and the possibility that your own reputation will be soiled will be minimized. Lastly, sex is always better when both parties are comfortable with each other and both parties feel that the proper time has arrived. It will not be rushed and neither party will be nervous. In addition, guys will tend not to say, "I have to get up early in the morning so I have to leave now that we are done." Girls will learn that guys will stay over if they are totally comfortable with the girl.

Why do guys like porno movies? Keep in mind that guys are stimulated more by visual things than by anything else. Watching pornos, by definition, is a visual thing for guys. They will become more aroused by watching naked women than they will by reading porno letters or talking to somebody.

Girls, on the other hand, are more emotional and kinesthetic. They will get more aroused from reading romantic stories or by taking warm, candlelit baths than they will be by watching porno movies. A guy can get a woman hot and bothered more easily by talking to her sexually than he could by showing her a porno movie.

Does it really matter what the partner does for a living? It really shouldn't, but of course it does. Guys probably care less about what their girlfriends do for a living than girls do. There are thousands of girls out there, and we all know a bunch of them, that attend certain colleges to get their MRS degree. There are also thousands of girls that will only marry a doctor, lawyer, or banker. These types of girls should be avoided at all costs because they are gold-digger girls who are as shallow as a puddle after a rainstorm. They also typically have absolutely no class and have nothing to offer you, so stay away.

Guys, on the other hand, really pay little attention to the career a woman has chosen. Several guys avoid girls, however, that are overly dedicated to their careers because they have no time for them. In addition, these girls may not want to have children because they are married to their careers.

When it comes to the actual career the woman has chosen, the man doesn't usually prejudge her. Most guys want to make sure that the girl does, however, have a career because he doesn't want her to quit her job and become a housewife the minute they start dating seriously. A guy wants his girlfriend to have a career that she enjoys and that is rewarding and profitable.

What do men like/dislike on dates? One common fallacy is that girls should not eat much on a first date. A girl tends to think that if she eats too much on a date that a guy will think she is rude, disgusting, or a glutton. Nothing could be further from the truth. When girls don't eat on a date, guys think that there is something wrong with them. A guy could think that he wasted his money on dinner because his date isn't eating. In addition, if she is pretending to be something other than herself now, it will only get worse. Girls, as well as guys, should be themselves at all times. After all, the guy asked out the girl he originally met, not the girl she is now pretending to be.

Guys like a lot of flexibility in their lives, and this is especially true when it comes to dates. While girls may think that a guy has made plans or reservations for the date days in advance (which is sometimes true), typically, he will decide what they are going to do on the date shortly before. Guys usually do not plan these things so far in advance, no matter what girls hope. In addition, guys want flexibility during the date. When I mention flexibility during the date, I don't mean that he will ask her to get naked and do a split (although he may ask her later). Instead, a guy will like to roll with the punches on the date. He may decide during the date to change plans or give the girl a choice of a number of different places to go after dinner. A girl may look at this and think that the guy didn't think about the date beforehand. This is not true. A guy is much more flexible than the girl, and would be happy going to a number of different places as long as he is with his date. He *has* thought about the date beforehand, but it really doesn't matter to him where they go afterwards.

Guys don't enjoy it very much, especially on the first few dates, if a girl meets one of her friends and invites them to spend dinner or the rest of the evening with them. Girls should realize that the guy asked them out, not their friends. And if that friend happens to be a guy (just a friend), the tension can be cut with a knife. No guy wants to have his date bring another guy to the dinner table or spend the rest of the evening with him and his date. The guy could feel threatened and think that his date doesn't want to spend time with him. The girl's intentions could be purely platonic, but it makes her date feel uncomfortable and should be avoided. Guys should heed the same advice.

A girl should not expect to have to pay for a date for at least the first three dates. A guy should pay for both parties for the first three. He should call her, make the plans, and pay for the date. However, after these three dates have been completed and the relationship continues, the girl should insist that she pays for something. Dating is not a one-way paying arrangement. Dating concerns two people that enjoy each other's company. When a guy pays all expenses of the dates, he begins to feel used. Any guy with self respect will not tolerate this situation too long. Guys will realize that this type of girl is only after their money and the situation will only get worse as the relationship progresses.

When the first date ends, the girl should not let the guy into her apartment. She should make sure that the guy is interested in more than just sex. Keep in mind that guys think with their penises and not their heads, especially when they drink. Also, keep in mind that sex for men is a lot less emotional than for women. If a guy didn't have fun on the date and doesn't plan to call her again, he may still try to get her in bed. Girls should realize this fact and not let them into their homes after the first date. If a guy wants her, he will call her again and make plans to go out again. Girls should let guys earn it. Too many girls have been hurt by guys just looking for sex on the first date.

Finally, if for some reason the girl gets sick or is tired and asks to go home early on a date, the guy should call her the next day to see how she is feeling. Even if he feels that she is going to blow him off, it is the right thing to do. Also, if the girl really was sick or tired, *she* should suggest getting together again. Girls should realize that the guy probably feels rejected and blown off and may not call again. If the girl wants to see the guy again, all she has to do is call, or even leave a message on his answering machine. This way, the guy will realize that she wants to see him again and that he hasn't been blown off.

What should a woman buy a guy as a gift? The best gift, and usually a very safe one, is clothing. Most guys do not like to shop, do not know where to buy the proper clothes, and do not have a keen sense of style. A nice blazer, sport shirt, or sweater is greatly appreciated by any guy. In fact, a great gift for a guy is a gift of custom-made shirts or suits for business. Guys need to dress for success, and nothing looks as good or feels as comfortable as custom-made business clothing. Introduce him to a tailor who can build shirts and suits for him. He can pick out his material from hundreds of different swatches and will never have to worry again that his suits or shirts don't fit.

Can you tell anything from the way he relates to his family? Absolutely. It is important to see how your girlfriend/boyfriend relates to their family. Are their parents still married? How do they relate to their siblings? How does the father treat the mother? Remember, this is the environment in which your girlfriend/boyfriend grew up. These are the relationships that formed during the formative and adolescent years. These are the types of relationships that can also be expected to be present in your relationship. If one's father has no respect for his wife, his son may have no respect for his future wife. If one's father is extremely protective and caring for his parents, one can expect the same type of behavior from the son. When people meet their girlfriend's/boyfriend's family, these things should be closely observed.

Can you learn anything from the magazines somebody reads? Sometimes. If a guy reads *BusinessWeek*, he is obviously in the financial field and is typically money-oriented. If he reads *Sports Illustrated*, he is a big sports fan and may want to stay in every Saturday night until the local basketball team plays. If he reads *GQ*, he has a good sense of fashion and self, and may be too self-involved. If he reads *Men's Health*, he obviously takes good care of himself and is more of a doer than a watcher.

Do guys like to go down on girls? Despite Krazee-Eyez Killa urging Larry David to do so, some guys do and some don't. Those that do will gladly do it whenever a girl wants him to do so. A girl is lucky if she finds such a guy, and there are a lot out there. Guys that do go down on girls realize how much better sex is when they do it. The best part about going down on a girl is the sexual pleasure that you are giving her. Guys that do it realize how important it is to make girls come and will stay down there until they do. The reactions of a girl who comes when you are down there are incredible, and get guys even more excited.

Besides, isn't it rude for guys not to do this? All guys expect girls to give them head and some, in fact, even push girls' heads down there. If a guy expects to have a girl do it, it is very selfish if guys don't do it too.

Can you tell anything from what a guy drinks? Sure, a lot can be concluded. When guys drink beer at dinner or a bar, they tend to be either young, immature, or just like to pound beer until the point that they get drunk. A quality girl isn't looking for this type of guy. And he may not be ready to meet a quality girl himself.

Guys that drink wine with women are typically the more romantic type. It is the type of alcohol most preferred by women and one they like to share with men. Can you imagine bringing a lady back to your home and asking her if she wants a beer? How unromantic.

Guys that drink Scotch, martinis, or cognac tend to be a little more mature and sophisticated than those guzzling beer at bars. They have found a drink they are comfortable with and are more at ease with themselves. They know what they like with respect to alcohol and they know what they like with respect to women. They are a little older, wiser, and able to form a lasting relationship.

What is in his refrigerator? Most eligible bachelors will have just the staples: beer, wine, vodka, salad dressing, soda, orange juice, water, and some microwaveable food. A girl looking into this fridge will realize that this guy usually doesn't cook for himself. He may order in food, go out a lot, or be very busy. If a guy has some salad, chicken, and vegetables, he could be apt to cook his own meals. Discreetly looking into a guy's fridge could yield many secrets to a curious girl.

Is searching through a guy's phone book an invasion of privacy? One of the worst things a girl could do! Who the hell is she to be searching through a guy's phone book? She isn't your wife! Several guys have ended relationships with girls because they caught them searching through their personal phone books. Besides, what the girl sees in the book is just an illusion anyway. She will instantly notice only the girls' names in the book and will automatically assume that the guy has slept with every one. She may even be foolish enough to ask the guy why he has so many girls' names in the book. Girls don't seem to realize that the guy had a very active life before they met and that he didn't stay home every Saturday night waiting for her to come along. He had an active dating life before the relationship, just like she did. She has to be comfortable enough in herself and the relationship to know that all of those girls are just friends or old girlfriends, who just happen to be there and mean little to him now. Keep in mind, girls, that it is you who is the object of the guy's desire now. Don't blow it by being jealous.

Does someone's dating history matter? Sure, especially nowadays with the increasing number of HIV positive people in every city. You should always find out a little bit about your intended love interest before you get sexually involved. I wouldn't recommend asking them detailed questions on the first date, but as the relationship progresses, you should be a little more inquisitive. Ask them if they have recently been tested for HIV. Don't be embarrassed to ask someone to take the test. They will gladly take it if they want to be sexually intimate with you. If they refuse, you are much better off not sexually involved with someone who has had sexual relationships with every other person in the county. Not only are you increasing your chances of getting diseases, but you want to avoid being with someone like that. They may be looking at you as Mr./Ms. Right Now as opposed to something special.

Do guys discuss sex with their friends? Not very often and sure as hell not as often as girls do. Guys really do not care whether their guy friends are sleeping with their girlfriends or about all of the details. They just care whether he enjoys spending time with her, or if he plans to date and sleep with other women. On the other hand, girls discuss the most intimate things about their boyfriends with several of their girlfriends. They claim not to do so, but when asked directly whether they do, they admit to doing so. They discuss their boyfriend's penis size, sexual proficiency, and whether he does "everything." Locker room chatter amongst guys ends in college, while it only begins for girls when they leave college. This may be the only area in which guys are more mature than girls at an earlier age.

Why do guys want to have boys' night out? Guys just like to do the things guys do. Go out, bullshit about stupid things, drink, talk about girls in general, talk sports, and chat about business. Since guys rarely talk to each other on the phone; it gives us a great opportunity to catch up. There are times when we prefer not to have the wife or girlfriend there because it is our special time to bond and just hang out. Girls have difficulty understanding this because they catch up with each other daily when they call each other on the phone. Girls are much more conversational than guys, especially on the phone, so we need our special time to bond with our guy friends.

What are the most important physical attributes that attract guys? Contrary to popular belief, there doesn't seem to be a universal answer to this question. Some guys are attracted by a girl's ass, some guys like legs, and others like big chests. Some men like curvy bodies while others prefer bigger women. Some like brunettes, some like blondes, and some like redheads. In fact, some guys will change their preferences over their lifetime. They may grow up liking blondes with big breasts, but later on be attracted to brunettes with long legs and small breasts.

However, the only universal theme is that the woman has a sense of sexuality. Guys like alluring women that ooze with sexuality. A playful glance, a parting of the hair, or an adoring or risqué touch can go very far. A woman should use her sexuality to keep a guy's interest.

Guys tend to like boobs. Why? Because we don't have them! We already have an ass, we like boobs. Many guys also like "fake boobs." I argue that boobs can't be "fake," they are "enhanced." Mickey Mouse is fake. You can't touch Mickey Mouse, but you can touch boobs!

Why aren't more guys romantic? Guys are just not that cognizant of a woman's feelings. Guys think more logically than girls do, and girls think more emotionally. It isn't that a guy doesn't care when he is not romantic. He may just not realize a woman's emotional needs or feelings. Girls should let guys know that it is greatly appreciated when guys compliment them, buy them flowers, or take them to romantic restaurants. If a guy is not as romantic as a woman would want him to be, she should talk to him about it before it gets to be a bad habit. Communication is the key to every relationship, so girls should let guys know what is on their minds.

Is it very important to have the same interests? Yes, I am sure. The theory that opposites attract is a fallacy. People who enter into a relationship will have to have a number of things in common or the relationship will not last. The more the couple has in common, the more time they can spend with each other doing things that both of them enjoy. It gives them more to talk about and more mutually enjoyable experiences. The relationship is a lot easier if both parties like similar foods, music, movies, and people. The less they have in common, the less likely the relationship will be successful.

Should women ever fake an orgasm? Not if she wants to keep her current boyfriend. Guys can usually tell when girls fake orgasms. If a guy has already slept with the girl before, he should be able to tell the difference between a fake and the real thing.

By faking an orgasm, the woman is only denying herself the real thing. Instead of faking it, why wouldn't she just communicate her needs more to the guy in question? The woman probably wouldn't have to fake any orgasm if she would only tell the guy exactly what gets her off. Trust me, girls, guys will be excited to hear about it.

In addition, if the guy ever suspected that the girl faked an orgasm, he would be devastated. Guys, by nature, have big egos and don't want to be humiliated by a girl who is in essence challenging his manhood by embarrassing him. A guy would much rather be told what he is doing wrong and what he should be doing than have a girl shatter his manhood by faking an orgasm.

What should a girl call her companion? This is a very important aspect of the relationship. When a girl introduces her man and vice versa, how the other person is referred to is crucial. When the relationship is relatively new, the other person can be referred to by just their name or by, "This is my friend, Brad." However, as the relationship progresses, this situation becomes a little stickier. Girls want to be called girlfriends before guys want to be called boyfriends. However, when the other person crosses the threshold to deserve girlfriend or boyfriend status is a difficult call. Typically, when the girl feels that she is now the guy's girlfriend, she will introduce you to people as such. The first time in the relationship that she does this will be a reality check for the guy.

Never refer to the other person as your lover. This terminology is sometimes used in Europe, but should always be avoided here. The only time people refer to each other as my lover is in Harlequin romance novels. The term is too risqué for people in this country. We all know that the two of you are sleeping with each other; we just don't want to hear about it or visualize it. In addition, could you imagine if you ever introduced your companion to your parents or grandparents and referred to them as your lover? I think my grandparents would have a heart attack.

What will guys do when their girlfriends get fat? Guys really hate it when their girlfriends get fat. They will lose interest very quickly and will even break up with girls just because they gain a few pounds. Guys should tell their girlfriends that they have gained a few pounds and that they should lose some weight. However, if they are afraid to tell their girlfriends, they may do one of the following things which will let the girl know that she should lose a few pounds.

A guy may take charge at a restaurant and order a salad for the girl instead of letting her order something for herself. Guys probably don't realize it, but girls will pick up on this very quickly. They become offended and may get into an argument at the dinner table. However, if she realizes that she needs to lose a few pounds, the objection should not last long. When girls recommend to a guy that he should eat less or better, it is taken to heart very quickly.

A more subtle way to approach the issue while at dinner is to tell the waiter, after he asks you whether you would like dessert, that the both of you definitely don't need it. This way you are saying that you don't need the extra fat yourself and she will not be offended.

A second thing that a guy may do is ask his girlfriend if she has been going to the gym. When he constantly asks her about whether she has worked out, she will begin to get the hint. It is a somewhat subtle way of telling your girlfriend that she needs to remember what the inside of a gym looks like.

Some guys may even be bold enough to buy their girl-friend a gym membership. This is also a tactful way of letting her know that you care and that you would like to see her work out and get into better shape.

Another thing that a guy may do is to recommend that they play tennis or go rollerblading together. This is a subtle way of letting her know that she should exercise more. This way may be the most tactful way because you will have fun doing it and spend more time with her. However, she may not get the hint.

Guys have also been known to throw out some fatty foods from the house or apartment. Girls will get the hint very quickly when they go searching for the bonbons, only to find that they have already been thrown down the garbage chute.

The best way, however, is to just come out and let her know that she would look much better if she lost weight. Confront her, but be tactful. Don't get mad at her, but instead you should let her know that you care a lot about her and would like to see her in better shape. Don't skirt the issue. Be direct. Perhaps you can suggest that the two of you should go on a diet and exercise program together. After all, you aren't that thin either!

Why do people talk about past relationships and boyfriends/ girlfriends? No matter what you think, one partner is always comparing the other to past boyfriends/girlfriends and past partners. It's human nature. However, the more you talk about past relationships, the more tension you will bring to the current relationship. Nobody wants to be compared to their partner's past boyfriends/girlfriends, especially if the comparison is unfavorable. Remember to keep past relationships where they belong, in the past.

VII. How Guys Can Make Themselves a Better Catch

There are dozens of things that all guys should be aware of with regards to dating and girlfriends. The following is a list of some of the ones I thought to be the most important. See if you agree with the following:

Get in shape. Work out. Lift weights, run, and exercise. You will not only look better, but you will feel better and have more energy and stamina. Most guys want to date girls with fabulous bodies, but don't work out themselves. Can you say double standard? Guys have no right to say that girls don't have nice bodies if they don't take care of their own.

When guys work out, they will also have a lot more self-confidence. They feel good about themselves and all of a sudden find themselves approaching girls that they never would have before. They may also meet girls at the gym or while running.

Go out. You will not meet anybody by watching television alone in your apartment. You can easily meet people doing things such as walking down the street or dropping off your dry cleaning. You have to network yourself and meet as many new people as possible. The only person you will meet by sitting in your apartment will be the delivery boy.

Call your friends and go to places where you will meet new people. Don't keep going to the same places because you will always see the same people. Try to go to places where you might know only a handful of people. You can talk with the people you know and ask them to introduce you to those you don't.

Meeting new people gets easier when you go to new places and do different things. It works like that old shampoo commercial whereby, "she told two friends, she told two friends ..." The more people you know, the more people you will meet. All of the new people will introduce you to new people and pretty soon, meeting new girls isn't that difficult any more.

Dress well. Girls notice guys when they dress well. You don't have to frequent Barney's on a daily basis to dress well. Shop intelligently and ask a girl whose fashion opinions you value to shop with you. Most guys hate clothes shopping anyway, so use the opportunity to meet girls at the same time. You may even ask an attractive girl for her opinion on an article of clothing you are considering.

Sloppy jeans and Pumas or Adidas T-shirts went out with Chuck Taylor's sneakers. Dress for the part. Dressing well will give you the confidence you need to meet new girls, and you will feel better about yourself.

As a rule of thumb, instead of dressing one level below the appropriate dress for the function you are attending, dress one level above. If the appropriate dress is for casual attire, wear a blazer and slacks. If the dress requirement is for a sport coat, wear a suit. You will stand out, look good, and have the confidence to meet new girls.

Speak well. Get rid of those annoying Midwestern, Long Island, or Boston accents. I made a conscious effort to lose my Long Island accent in college when a girl whom I had just met said, "So, where in Long Island are you from?" I became very aware of my accent thereafter and lost it gradually over the next few months.

If you have to, go to a speech counselor. Think about how you sound with those annoying accents. Listen to your telephone answering machine message to hear yourself speak. If you only use twenty-five letters of the alphabet (Long Island accents do not use an *r* at the end of spoken words), you better (not *betta*) start working on your accent.

Check the spelling of some of the words you use. There is no such word as *aks*, *yous*, or *supposebly*. The proper spelling is *ask*, *you*, and *supposedly*. When somebody says the word *yous* to you, you should invariably say, "Excuse me, *use* is a verb. Please use it that way!"

People judge the intelligence of people initially by the way they speak. If you speak with a bad accent or with improper words, others will not believe you to be too intelligent. Don't buy into this Ebonics or Jewbonics shit. Whenever you hear the phrases "He be at the store" or "Oh … my … God," you just can't help but think that this person is a fucking idiot.

Read the newspaper every day. Educate yourself. Know what is happening in the world. Develop opinions. It is important to be aware of current events. Have intelligent discussions with people about stories in the news. People will consider you to be intelligent.

Guys get turned off by really stupid women just as much as women are turned off by stupid men. Who wants to date somebody who thinks the Middle East is just east of cities in the Midwest?

Girls love intelligent men. They are extremely attracted to them. They say that intelligence is one of their biggest turn-ons. Most girls like the character Chandler (Matthew Perry) on *Friends* because he is the smart and witty one. Girls look at Joey (Matt Le Blanc) as an idiot. Most girls would have chosen Joey as their favorite friend when they were young, but mature girls prefer Chandler.

Vary your interests. While sitting on the couch and watching football all day can be fun, sports can't be your sole interest. See a movie. Go to a museum. Read a book. Take a class at a college or school. Take up a hobby. Learn to play a new sport. Whatever you like, learn to do new things. Try to be a Renaissance man.

Not only will you become more well-rounded, but you may meet some interesting people along the way. You will already have something in common to talk about because they are doing the same thing that you are. Varying your interests and doing new things is a great way to meet new people.

Have a *positive attitude* about things. Never doubt yourself. If you are tentative when meeting a girl, she will pick up on it and sense your apprehension. Always believe that good things will happen, and that girls will like you just the way you are.

When you walk around with self-doubt or with the feeling that you are unlucky, you will not succeed at anything. Always believe that things will be great even when things look bad. Hard work and confidence will be your tools for success. People that are lucky tend to be the ones that have worked the hardest.

If you have self-doubt, look at yourself in the mirror every day and tell yourself that you are great. Do this especially when you are depressed or have had a bad day at work or socially. It sounds kind of corny, but it works. Don't leave that mirror until you believe that you will make things better. Then go out and *make* them better.

Keep in mind, however, that there is a fine line between confidence and cockiness. My friend from the University of Pennsylvania, Mark Saunders, said it best: "Cockiness is knowing what you can do, while confidence is knowing what you have to do."

Don't be afraid to approach a new girl. If you don't, you will be kicking yourself in the ass all night for not doing so. Go out of your way to meet her. You have nothing to lose. The worst thing that will happen is that she won't talk to you. So, instead of feeling like you didn't give it a shot, you realize that even though she is very attractive, she isn't for you.

Listen and empathize with girls. You have to realize that girls are more emotional than guys. You have to understand this and allow them to express themselves to you. Be cognizant of what you say because they may believe you said one thing, even though you meant it another way. Tell her how you feel and try to understand how she feels.

Everybody likes to talk about themselves so allow the girl to tell you about herself. You already know about yourself, don't you want to know more about her? If you are looking for a smart, intelligent girl, you must allow her to talk. Everybody feels more comfortable with people after they have been talking about themselves. It is strange, but true. Think about it. Don't you feel more comfortable with someone after you have just told them about yourself? Realistically, they should feel more comfortable with you, but that's not the way it works.

Never tell anybody whom you are dating when the relationship is not yet serious. Your friends will keep asking about her, and if the new relationship doesn't work out, you will find yourself explaining the situation to all of your friends. You are better off just telling them that you are dating people, but nobody serious. Should you date this person about five or six times, then you may want to let your friends know what you have been doing the last few weekend nights.

In addition, should you plan on dating more than one girl at a time, it is in your best interests not to tell anybody about either one. The more people that know about your situation, the greater chance that somebody will open up their big mouth about it and ruin your situation. People frequently date more than one person at a time early in a relationship, so it is not too wise to let the world know what you are doing.

Never tell anybody how sexually involved you get with any girl. It is nobody else's business besides the two people involved. You should never tell your friends about how involved you get with girls, even if you don't talk to the girl anymore. What difference does it make to your friends if you slept with this girl or only kissed another girl?! You should look at it as an infringement upon your privacy and avoid being asked about it. Grow up, guys. You have nothing to prove to your friends. Trust me, it doesn't make you a bigger person in their eyes when you tell them how far you got with last night's date. It really makes you look like a sleazy, immature, insecure asshole.

Personal grooming is very important. Make sure you complete the three S's before you see her: shit, shower, and shave. The girl will think that you don't care about her when you show up sloppy. Also, remember to trim your nose hairs. Not only will they cause a terrible tickle in your nose which may cause you to sneeze, they are unsightly. Girls do not like to see hair growing out of your nose and ears. Invest in a nose hair trimmer or cuticle scissors and cut away. Trimming the hair is a lot less painful than yanking them out, and doesn't cause your eyes to tear.

Make sure your hair is clean and well-cut. Put on some aftershave after you shave, but not too much. Check your clothes to see if they are properly pressed and check to see if your shoes are shined. Finally, make sure your clothes are color coordinated and the color of your belt matches the color of your shoes. If you are color-blind, you will need to have somebody match them for you.

Be prompt. If you tell her that you are going to pick her up at 9:00 PM, be there at 9:00 PM. Girls are always running late. It annoys guys when girls are late, but there is not much we can do about it. Girls like it very much when guys are always on time, even though they are always late. Perhaps, if you show her that punctuality is important to you, she will start being more punctual.

Should your relationship progress to the point that you are spending a lot of time with the girl, you may have to tactfully speak to her about her chronic lateness. Try to avoid a major confrontation, but you should be firm with her and let her know that a few minutes here and there is no big deal, but she always seems to be thirty to forty-five minutes late and that is unacceptable. Tell her that it is important to be on time most of the time. If it doesn't work, you will just have to tell her to be ready fifteen to twenty minutes earlier every time you go out.

Remember birthdays and anniversaries. They are very important to girls and an important part of any relationship. Wouldn't you feel bad if your girlfriend didn't make a big stink about your birthday? Now, if we have already agreed that girls are more emotional than guys, wouldn't it reason that she would feel even worse if you didn't remember her birthday?

Anniversaries are just as important. Girls will fall for a guy who remembers the anniversary of their first date and any other significant anniversaries. You will win a lot of brownie points for remembering your anniversaries.

The gifts you give to her or the place you take her for birthdays or anniversaries should be special. Don't take her to that fancy new French restaurant called Le Chateau Blanc (White Castle). Take her to her favorite restaurant or one to which she has always wanted to go. Buy her flowers for your anniversary and tell her that you love her. These things are very important to women. Treat her like gold every day, but treat her like a queen on her birthday and anniversary.

Send things *impromptu*. You do not need a reason to send flowers or little gifts. Doing so is a sure sign that you are thinking about her and that she means a lot to you. Think about the significance of the gift before you send it. The gift you send should have some special significance for the both of you.

You should also call her impromptu and tell her that you love her. Try calling her at work or texting her cell phone to tell her that you had nothing new to say, but just wanted to tell her that you love her and/or miss her. Watch the attention and love you'll get that evening.

Be polite. Avoid cursing and being vile or overly sexually explicit, especially early in the relationship. It makes you look crude, boorish, and too blue collar. And never, ever, use the "C" word. You know the one. It rhymes with what pitchers do with a man on first and no out, or what football teams do on fourth and long. Girls hate this word, and they will let you know it. Not only is that word to be avoided in conversation, never use it in bed. It is not seen as a term of endearment for that part of the anatomy. Guys have been known to be thrown out of bed for using that word.

In addition, be polite with people you encounter in your daily lives. A girl will not enjoy seeing you curse out a waiter no matter how inefficient he may be. Instead, frequent use of the words *please* and *thank you* are appropriate. Girls would always rather be dating a gentleman than a boor.

Romance is extremely important in relationships. Try not to lose the romance from a relationship because it is very hard to recover. Girls are very attracted to romantic men, so if you want to be their love interest, learn to be romantic. No, you don't have to write her love poetry every day, but an occasional letter wouldn't hurt. Tell her that you love her and miss her when you are away from her. Leave messages on her machine telling her that you were thinking about her if you haven't seen her for a while (think of Billy Joel's "Tell Her About It").

Lack of romance is a big reason for disappointing relationships. If you care about someone enough, you should show them. Don't ever take a girl for granted because she will start looking elsewhere. Most guys have learned this lesson once during their lives and will probably not repeat the mistake. Girls are more prone to having an affair when they feel unloved or that the romance has left the relationship.

Hold the door for your lady. It sounds so simple, but a lot of guys don't do it. Holding the door for a lady should be instinctive. You should also open the car door on the passenger side to let your date into your car before you enter. Don't open your door first, get in, and open her door from the inside. It is such a small thing to do, but it is the right thing to do, and shows a sense of respect for your girlfriend.

Also hold the door for other people and give up your seat on the bus or subway, especially for older people. Not only is it the right thing to do, but the more good gentlemanly habits you form, the more attractive you are to women.

Always pay for the first few dates. Even if she insists, tell her that you will allow her to pay when and if she asks you out. If she never even asks to pay, then you have a potential problem. Don't ever get involved with a girl who never offers to pay. It is rude and shows you that she is a spoiled brat. I had a couple of situations like this over the past few years and each time found the girl to be a c--t (sorry, girls). Every girl that I have ever dated seriously has never even thought twice about offering to pay. Just don't let them pay for the first few dates. If they choose to pay once in a while thereafter, that is fine.

When you start dating a girl, don't leave a message on her machine saying that you called. You should always make sure you speak to her directly. She may not be inclined to call you back because she wants you to pursue her a little and be a little less lazy. Girls will sometimes not call you back after the first or second date if you just leave a message because they don't think it was appropriate for you to just leave a message.

If you feel that you must leave a message, say something like, "I had a great time last night and would like to see you again. I will call you later." Never leave a message such as, "Hi, it's me, call me back." She typically won't. She wants to feel special and wants to see you make an effort. She realizes that if you want her badly enough, you will call back.

When you have sex with the girl at her apartment, always spend the night and always call the next day. If you don't, you will make the girl feel like a tramp and she will feel used. You will have difficulty justifying your departure. Sex is a more emotional experience for women than it is for men. Most women will only sleep with you when they have feelings for you. Guys tend to be able to fuck anything in sight. Thus, if the girl is emotionally tied to you, you better spend the night if you ever want to see her again.

Don't use the excuse that you have to get up early in the morning. Girls will see right through it and not believe you. If you do have to get up early the next morning, make the date on a night where you don't. Also, if you are going to sleep at a girl's apartment for the first time, you have to stay until at least 7:00 AM, or else she will start throwing shoes at you as you leave. Don't ruin the experience by being an asshole.

The next day you have to call her and tell her that you had a great time the night before. You can't wait two days before calling her, even if that was your calling pattern before you slept with her. She is feeling a little vulnerable and insecure, hoping that you didn't use her. She wants to know that you care about her and that all of the things you said to her to get her in bed are true. It doesn't matter where you are or what you are doing, you have to call her to allay her fears. If she isn't home, leave a message telling her that you had a great time, want to see her again, and will call her again later.

Try to pick her up at her apartment. Avoid meeting her at a place if possible. She will feel better about you and respect you more if you make the effort to come to her apartment to get her. If you continue to meet her at places, she will think that you are lazy and really don't care about her. Treat her like a lady by picking her up and walking her to her door after the date.

Once again, you have to be a gentleman. Tolerate her lateness at first. Compliment her on her apartment. Tell her that she looks great. Tell her that you were looking forward to seeing her.

Eat well. You will feel better and look better. Avoid fatty foods such as cheeseburgers, chicken wings, bacon, butter, and pizza. Eat lighter and less. Your body needs less food as you get older, and it is easier to feel bloated when you eat too much.

If you have to, ask your doctor or a trainer at your gym to put you on a loose diet. They are experts on nutrition and will work with you to establish a workable diet that you will be able to follow.

In addition, more and more girls are eating better and it doesn't look good to her if she eats a salad and you order a heart-attack sandwich. She probably wants her boyfriend to eat as well as she does.

Don't smoke. This is the single most disgusting habit somebody can have. Many guys don't even date girls that smoke. They smell, they are unhealthy, and they are not a joy to kiss. Smoking makes your clothes and hair smell and makes your teeth brown. This is not an ideal date.

If you are currently dating a girl that smokes, you have to make every effort to try to break her habit. Start by sitting down with her and telling her how much you care about her and that you are concerned for her health. Tell her that you are really turned off by the habit and that you will work with her to break the habit. If you care about her enough, you will have success.

Compromise is an important part of any relationship. You can't always do what you want when you are in a relationship. Sometimes you have to go to your girlfriend's Aunt Shirley's party even though you would rather jerk off with a sandpaper glove while lying on a bed of nails. Grow up. It's part of the relationship. Trust me; she hates your cousins from Harrisburg, too.

Rest assured that she may not always want to go to the football game with you (how sacrilegious!). That's fine, just take one of your friends and agree to take her to her favorite restaurant when you get home. Compromise is one of the true building blocks of the relationship. Work at it. You will get more things that you want anyway.

Never take her for granted. If you do, she may not be around too long. Keep in mind that you are not the only one who finds her attractive and appealing. If you do not spend quality time with her and show her that you love her, she will be gone faster than Usain Bolt running the two hundred meters.

It is important to remember that if you want to make her your girlfriend or your wife, she has to become the most important part of your life. Do what it takes to let her know that she is loved and appreciated. Thank her for the special things she does for you and let her know how important she is to you.

If you own a dog, use it to your advantage. Walking your dog can be a fantastic way to meet girls. Get a dog that girls will like. Don't get a poodle or a chow. Only ritzy women and effeminate men like poodles and chows. Get a fun dog that girls will like to play with. Take the dog to the park and just walk around. Girls will flock to you like flies to shit. It is such an easy way to meet girls.

If you do not want to own a dog, borrow one of your friends' dogs. I'm sure that you have lots of friends with dogs. Several married couples seem to be getting dogs in lieu of having children while they are newlyweds. Ask one of them to borrow their dog. They will be happy to let you walk it, and they will be the first to let you know how dogs can be chick magnets.

However, never believe the theory that dogs are man's best friends. Your best friend doesn't stop to smell shit on the sidewalk. Your best friend doesn't try to hump a guy's leg. Your best friend doesn't leave his head outside of the car window when traveling over fifty miles per hour. Your best friend doesn't walk outside and piss on a fire hydrant in subzero temperatures. Your best friend doesn't shit on the floor of the apartment when he can't go outside. Your best friend doesn't lick his own penis in public (well, maybe he would if he could). Your best friend doesn't sniff another person's genitals in public as they pass by (at least, I hope they don't).

And speaking of pets, *don't buy a snake.* Girls hate snakes. Snakes aren't interesting pets because they don't do anything. Some guys like to parade around their neighborhood with their pet snake wrapped around their necks. Trust me, guys, very few girls find snakes even vaguely appealing.

Picture this: A guy takes his girlfriend to the pet store to get food for his pet snake that hasn't eaten in two months. He asks his girlfriend to pick out a nice, juicy mouse that he can feed to his pet. Do you really think that any sane girl is going to find this scenario stimulating?

If you are bald, don't hide it. What's the big deal? Do you really think that ladies find it attractive when men have coast-to-coast haircuts (those that are combed from one side of the head all of the way to the ear on the other side of the head)? Similarly, do you really think that ladies like summer haircuts (some are here and some are there)? You aren't fooling anybody and it looks ridiculous.

Be proud if you are bald. A lot of women find baldness to be very sexy. Yul Brynner, Telly Savalas and Michael Jordan all have done very well with the ladies. In addition, Mr. Clean did very well with the babes, too. Why do you think he has that big smile on his face?

Change your sheets if you expect to have a home game (have a lady sleep over). Girls don't want to sleep in dirty sheets and would prefer to see your bed when it is made before you get under the covers. In addition, if you happen to have had another girl stay over on a previous night, not that I am promoting that, a girl will be very sensitive to another girl's perfume and scent. If you haven't changed your sheets after your first encounter, the new girl will be able to smell the first girl's perfume and may even find a hair in the bed that doesn't belong to her. Avoid this embarrassing situation and change the sheets.

You must also clean your hairbrush, sink, and tub. If a girl was in your apartment recently, she has used your brush to comb her hair and may have even showered in your tub. If a second uses your bathroom, she will find long hairs all over the place. You will have a hard time explaining why there are long blonde hairs all over your bathroom when your new date is a brunette.

Don't order in too often. If you want to meet girls, ordering food up to your apartment when you are alone is not the way to do it. If you are ordering food, go out to pick it up. At least you have a chance of meeting someone in your building, at the restaurant, or on the way to the restaurant. I do not know too many guys that eventually date the Domino's delivery boy!

Learn to recognize different perfumes. Girls love guys that can identify their perfume. If a girl is wearing your favorite perfume, tell her how much you like it. Personally, I can recognize about five different perfumes and am very attracted to Alfred Sung perfume. I find it hard to control myself around beautiful girls that wear that perfume. If you have to go to a store and smell perfumes, do it. You may even meet an attractive girl at the counter. Learn about all of the perfumes that your girlfriend has and determine which you like the best.

If you don't like her perfume, don't be afraid to let her know. Bad perfume can ruin a relationship for no serious reason outside of the fact that you hate it. Tell her, if you want to be sensitive about it, that you are allergic to her current perfume and ask her to change. You may also casually suggest some other perfumes with which you are familiar.

Don't eat onions or peppers the day of or during your date. Your breath will smell something awful and she might not want to kiss you. Just avoid eating them and your date will be more fruitful.

Also, do not eat any foods that day which will upset your stomach. You have been looking forward all week to going out with this girl, why spend it in the bathroom all night (especially with no reading material to at least make the experience enjoyable)?

When in a new relationship, *do not take a girl out to dinner across the street from her apartment.* It shows no imagination and that you did not put any thought into your date. She has already eaten there a dozen times with her friends, so why would she want to go there again on your date? Keep in mind that you are supposed to be going out, not across.

When in a new relationship, *never take a girl out to dinner across the street from your apartment.* Guess what, guys? Girls aren't that stupid. They know what you are trying to do. You just want to take them to dinner, not see anybody you know, get them trashed, and then invite them to your apartment to do the wild thing. Even if you are planning to take her back to your place to get laid, at least take her out to a restaurant away from your place of residence.

Clean your toilet and tub. Keep in mind that the girl may end up staying over and will invariably use the toilet and the shower. Make sure that both are spotless. Your bathroom is a reflection upon you and should always be kept clean. Girls are more finicky when it comes to clean bathrooms, so if you want them to come to your apartment, clean up your facilities.

Be independent before you are dependent. In other words, you can't add anything to a relationship until you are comfortable with yourself and can live on your own. Relationships are difficult and should be approached cautiously. You must have some idea of what you want out of life before you can attempt to share it with someone else. If you are not established with your career, or even if you still aren't sure what it is you should be doing in life, you will not be able to give enough of yourself to have a fulfilling relationship. It is important to get your house in order before you can proceed with a mature relationship.

The reverse is true for women, as well. Don't get involved with a girl that does not have any idea of what she wants out of life. You don't want to get married to a girl and one day get home from work one day to find her knitting, eating Milk Duds, and watching *Saved By the Bell*.

Try to go out socially with only two other guys. This will allow you to meet more ladies. For example, if you are at a cocktail party and one of your friends meets another woman, you are not forced to talk to her friend (in other words, you are not required to take one for the team) if you are not interested because there is another guy to help you out. It is much easier to politely walk to the bar to get a drink if one of your friends is there.

Also, if you are out to dinner with two other guys, you will always have an extra chair at your table. Should one of your friends know a girl at the restaurant, she can come to your table and sit at the guest chair instead of standing over you as you eat. It makes it far easier to meet a girl and her friends, should she be with anybody that interests you.

Always carry a business card with you. You never know when you will meet a girl in a situation that will only allow you to speak for a few moments before one of you has to leave. Make sure you have that business card ready to give to her and make sure you tell her you would like to take her to lunch the next day when you give it to her. Even if you already have lunch plans the whole week, make it sound like you are free to take her to lunch the next day. This will put the ball in her court to call you sooner than later, should she decide to call. When she does call and you tell her that you are busy, apologize and say that you had a meeting scheduled that you had forgotten about. Ask her out for lunch during one of your free days.

You can also give your business card to a waiter at a restaurant to give to a girl with whom you've been flirting, or to one of the girl's friends if your love interest has already left. Make sure you carry a few cards whenever you are out socially, and make sure that your work phone number and address is legible.

Have some self-respect. Not every girl is going to like you and all guys get blown off once in a while. If you ask a girl out and she declines, she may be busy. If she is interested in you, I have found that she will recommend another time or another date. If not, she may just say no thank you. Guys can probably ask out a girl two times without success before he should cut his losses and realize she is not interested. Don't continue to call! You are only serving to harass her and you are losing your self-respect. Forget her! There are dozens of other girls out there that you should be pursuing. If she doesn't want to go out with you, she is not worth your time. Go out with the boys and get back on the prowl.

Be careful when dating an only child. They might be spoiled brats because their parents gave them everything they ever wanted while growing up. They sometimes can be mal-adjusted because they did not grow up with any siblings. Girls who have brothers and/or sisters tend to be more stable.

Always return phone calls. It is the right thing to do and you sure as hell don't like it when your calls aren't re-turned. If you are not returning a call because you are trying to avoid somebody, you are only doing both of you a disservice. Since you eventually have to speak with that person to resolve the situation, you might as well take care of it as soon as possible and not let it fester.

This credo is valid for both business and social instances. It is always better to run through your problems rather than around them. If you face your problems head-on, it will be a lot easier to get rid of them instead of letting them fester. Don't avoid problems because they will only get worse. Attack them and get rid of them. You will rest a lot easier at night.

Honesty, as they say, is the best policy. Don't lie to girls because it will invariably come back to haunt you. We don't like to be lied to, so why should we lie to them? If you want to break up with your girlfriend, tell her immediately that you just don't feel the way she does and move on. It is best for both parties. If you feel slighted by something some girl did, tell her about it. Honesty is the cornerstone for every relationship.

Call within two days of taking a new girl's phone number. Don't play games. If you want to go out with her, show her by calling soon. The longer you wait, the more she is convinced that you really don't care. Even if you are not yet able to set your first date, call to say hello and to begin to get to know her. It is very important.

If you wait too long, she will forget about you. A lot of guys like to wait five or six days to call a new girl. This theory should quickly be abandoned and forgotten. A girl always wants to feel special. If you like her or think you like her, call within two days. Set the stage early that there is no bullshit about you and that you don't play games.

Try to avoid talking about ex-girlfriends and ex-boyfriends. Your new love interest may already be intimidated by your memory of them or even worse, will feel awkward when meeting them. You will only do damage to your current relationship by referring to old boyfriends and girlfriends. Nobody wants to continuously hear about their current flame's exes.

Never, ever compare your ex with your current relationship. This is just about the worst thing you can do and will lead to a quick end to your relationship. Everybody and every relationship is different. Sure, there are a lot of things that you liked about your previous boyfriends and girlfriends, but there are also a lot of things you like about your new flame. Instead of comparing your ex and your current relationship, you should:

Compliment your girlfriend. Girls love compliments and want to know that you notice them and what they wear and do. Pay attention to this, guys. It is a very important aspect of your relationship. Tell her that she looks beautiful. Tell her that you like her outfit. Tell her that she is wearing your favorite perfume. Tell her that you enjoy spending time with her mother (so big deal, you lie once in a while). Compliments will help you develop a lasting and secure relationship. Just make sure that they are sincere.

Try to enjoy some of the things that she enjoys. It will come to benefit you the most. Trust me. She will be so thrilled that you spend time with her doing things she enjoys that she will go overboard to enjoy the things you would like to do.

Don't introduce a girlfriend to your family too soon. Try to avoid having her meet the parental units too soon, and definitely avoid introducing her to the grandparents. An introduction to the grandparents bestows upon her head the title girlfriend. If the relationship doesn't work and you have introduced her to your family, they will harass you incessantly about why you broke up. Your grandparents have already told all of their friends at the bridge club that you are getting married and have begun dress and suit shopping. They may even start to get their designated outfits out of the mothballs.

Make sure that you are comfortable with your new girlfriend before you introduce her to the family. In fact, you should actually be referring to her as your girlfriend long before even thinking about introducing her to your family.

Of course, if you haven't had any significant relationships for a while and haven't introduced any girl to your family for a long time, they may start to tease you about being gay or start asking you to get married before they die. Don't give in! Wait for your princess. She will come, but you have to kiss a lot of frogs before you meet her. In fact, I'm sure some of the frogs that you have kissed haven't been so bad either!

Don't leave your belongings in her apartment too soon. This will cause problems retrieving your things when and if you break up. Make sure that the relationship is somewhat stable before you start leaving things at her apartment and vice versa.

In addition, leaving things at her apartment may leave the impression with her that you are very serious about the relationship, when, in reality, you may not be yet. You should not leave things at her apartment, except maybe some hangout clothes and some toiletries, before you are good and ready. Be careful when using toiletries in her bathroom. After a late night out, I once tried to brush my teeth in the dark only to find out that I had put Vagisil on my toothbrush.

Make friends with your doorman. They are a great asset to you when it comes to dating. They can make you aware of girls coming to your apartment and they have to make sure that, if you are dating more than one girl, they do the right thing and don't blow it for you.

Doormen are also great resources for meeting people in your building. If you see a girl in your building that you want to meet, you can ask the doormen about her. Rest assured that they know more about her than they should. They know whom and if she is dating, they know what time she comes home at night and in what condition, and they know what kind of person she is. Ask your doorman for a synopsis and ask them to introduce you. It is a very easy and non-threatening introduction.

Don't play your answering machine messages in front of your date. There is always that possibility that some other girl, maybe a current date or ex-girlfriend, may have left a message on the machine which should only be heard by you. Make sure that the volume is on the lowest level when there is a girl in your apartment. The worst thing that could happen is that you are fooling around with a girl, the phone rings, the machine picks it up, and you both then hear another girl tell you on the machine that she wants to see you or that she had a great time with you last night. Be smart; avoid the problem and keep the volume low.

Don't date a girl older than you are. This especially applies when you are in your late twenties or early thirties. Girls tend to feel the urgency to get married faster at those ages than guys do. When you date a younger girl, the relationship is more relaxed.

When in doubt about how young you can date, refer to the following formula: 1/2 your age + 7. You can date girls that are older than the formula. If you are thirty-two, you can date girls twenty-three and older. When guys are on vacation, however, the formula changes somewhat. The new age becomes: 1/2 your age + 3. Anything goes on vacation, especially if it is far away from home and the likelihood of seeing the girl again is slim.

Don't date girls that have more facial hair than you do. This causes a problem as to who gets to shave first in the morning. Guys don't like their dates using their Gillette Sensor to shave their facial hair. So, instead of telling them not to touch the razor, don't date girls with facial hair.

Don't date a girl who can dunk over you or weighs more than you. When you get married, you would rather carry your bride over the threshold, not the other way around. When you walk down the street with a girl, you would prefer that she not be called "Butch" or "Rocky" by people walking down the street.

Try to avoid dating girls in your own building. It will only cause problems with regard to the pace of the relationship. She will want to spend all her time with you, which is fine if you are ready for that. If not, you will feel cornered and the relationship will end.

Dating a girl in your building will also cause problems if one of you catches the other on a date with another. Early on in relationships, one party or the other is probably dating more than one person. Should the other person see their current dating interest with another person, it will make the situation awkward, even though it may mean nothing. You are better off avoiding this situation.

Don't let people tell you that you are too picky. Don't let them tell you that you have to compromise what you are looking for. Your dream girl with almost all of the attributes that you find to be important will eventually come along. Don't ever settle! You will not be happy and you will only be wasting your time. Don't let the pressure from your parents or grandparents make you make a decision to marry someone when you are not ready.

If you are going to ask a girl out on the weekend, try to do it at least three days in advance. She is not going to revolve her life around you, just like you won't revolve your life around her. Have some respect for her time. She wants to spend time with you, but you have to let her know that you are thinking about her in advance. She wants to spend time with her friends just like you do. Don't disrespect her and take her for granted. Remember, there are other guys that will ask her out.

Be wary of girls that ask you how much money you make. What difference does it make? This shouldn't be a major factor in a relationship, especially early in the dating process. A girl should like you for yourself and not how big your wallet is. Similarly, don't you want to like a girl for herself and not for her salary? Of course, more money is better than no money, but this should not be the deciding factor for a date. Look at money as the icing on the cake. The cake would still taste great without icing, but it sure tastes a lot better with it!

Take your time before having sex for the first time in a relationship. If you plan on having a serious relationship with a girl, it shouldn't really matter how long you wait to have sex for the first time. Trust me, if you wait, the girl will be insatiable. She will appreciate it so much that you'll get more play than you could ever imagine!

In addition, the relationship will last longer. She will respect you more and trust you more. She feels special and important and this will sustain the relationship. The sex will be better when you wait anyway. If one or both of you are not ready, the sex will be awkward and you may not feel that both of you are getting everything you can out of it. Remember that females are very emotional and will bond with you more sexually when they are emotionally ready to have sex.

Also, if you have sex too early in the relationship and you then break up, you will have damaged her emotionally because she will feel used. You, although you had a brief moment of pleasure, will also feel as if you used her. Better to wait until both of you are sure you want to proceed with the relationship.

Moving in with a girl should only be done if you are doing it as a test before engagement. Unless you plan on getting engaged to this girl in the near future, don't move into her place or allow her to move into your place. If you have no plans on marrying this girl, you are living with someone for the wrong reasons. Once you move in with a girl, you are basically telling her that this is a trial before engagement. If you are not sure about whether you want to marry this girl, you shouldn't live together.

Don't have an affair with a married woman. You will only be causing problems for yourself because she may become attached to you, especially if her marriage is falling apart. Though you may feel that having an affair is sex without the strings attached, you are wrong. She may leave her husband for you and expect to date you exclusively. Then what? You've achieved the result that you never thought would happen. You are now dating a girl who thinks you are her boyfriend and you are the cause of a divorce.

In addition, you are hurting the girl's husband. I'm sure that if you had problems with your marriage, you wouldn't want your wife to have an affair. So, why is this case any different? If they get divorced, then feel free to go out with her. She will be less possessive and you will not be the cause of the divorce.

After you break up with your girlfriend (or vice versa), never stay in your apartment and mope. If you do, you will rot. You must keep your mind off of the situation and focus on other things. If you go home after work and stay in your apartment, you will find yourself lying on your bed staring at the ceiling. There are other things you should be doing with your time to keep your mind off of the ex-burden.

Get more involved at work. Try to avoid the down times at work by working harder and taking on more responsibility. Keep your eye on the ball and get more focused. You will have more time on your hands now that you aren't dating the ball-and-chain any longer, so use your time productively.

Spend more time with your friends. Your friends have always counted on you during a pinch so now it is time to return the favor. Good friends will keep your mind off of your ex.

Work out more. Relieve your stress by working out more and harder. Your body will feel better, and thus you will feel better mentally. Transfer your stress from your mind to the weights.

You live only once so take advantage of life. Unless you are Shirley MacLaine, you are only on this planet once. And unless you are Elizabeth Taylor, you only have one period of being single. You have very few responsibilities when you are single. You don't have to tell a wife that you are going away with the boys for the weekend, nor do you have to run home after work to take Junior to the doctor. Enjoy life! Do fun and exciting things. Travel. Take advantage of being single. Don't be afraid to approach new girls because the only thing they can do that would be bad is that they tell you no.

Give up closet space and drawers when your girlfriend moves in. After all, this is now going to be where both of you are living. She isn't just staying for the weekend. Show her that you really want her to be there and make accommodations for her.

In addition, give her extra bathroom space and medicine cabinet space. Girls use much more room in the bathroom than guys do. They tend to have several bags of makeup, pills, and hair dryers, so let them have their space. The bathroom is one of a girl's favorite places. If it wasn't, why would they spend so much time in there?

Have at least one Barry White CD in your CD collection.
I went to my first Barry White concert in the summer of
1996 and have never seen a man have such an effect on
women as big Barry did. I became a fan many years ago
and have had great success with women while listening to
the late, great Barry White.

Always have a bottle of white wine in the refrigerator. You
never know when you will have a guest over to your
apartment. Make sure it is properly chilled and your wine
glasses are clean. Girls do not want to be asked if they
want to have a beer. Wine is romantic and very conducive
to getting intimate.

Don't ever leave two wine glasses in the sink. Girls will not
think anything of you leaving other glasses in the sink, especially if the rest of your apartment is clean. However, if
she finds two dirty wine glasses in the sink and she hasn't
been in your apartment for a while, guess what? You're
nailed! She knows that you have recently had another girl
in your apartment and that you have been in each other's
arms. Girls aren't that naive and they are very observant.
Any other type of glass in the sink, and she doesn't think
twice. Two wine glasses, and you might as well have come
out and told her that you were naked with another girl the
previous night. She knows that two guys will never drink
wine together in one of their apartments.

Attain a proper balance in life. Don't neglect any aspect
of your life. Your life encompasses many things and you
should make time in your life for all of them.

Work hard and take on new challenges at the office. Strive for promotion and new responsibilities. Develop strong business and personal relationships with people at work.

Play hard and always look to enjoy yourself. You work hard all day so you deserve to relax and have fun. Develop the ability to laugh at yourself. Don't always take yourself too seriously. If you can't laugh at yourself, you can't laugh at anything or anybody else.

See your friends and take an active role in their lives. Allow them to be an integral part of your life. Friends are important and will always be there for you. If you can't always get to see them, pick up the phone. Find out what is happening in their lives. Ask them about work, mutual friends, and relationships. Learn to care about other people, too.

See your girlfriend. Build a relationship. Allow it to mature. Find out as much as you can about her because one day you may decide to spend the rest of your life with her. Try to have profound conversations and determine her opinions, beliefs, and fears.

Spend time with your family. Family is very important. You are lucky if you have a close family. Not everybody does. Take the time to know about your parents and grandparents because they are the major part of your roots, and they will not be around forever. Become closer with your siblings. I am lucky to have a brother who has become my best friend and parents who have always taken a great deal of interest in their two children, and who have dedicated a great deal of time making sure that their children are happy. I wish a family like mine upon all.

Spend time with yourself. Read a book or work out. Watch television or listen to music. You spend so much time with others that it is important to get to know yourself and relax.

VIII. Conclusion

We are all continuing to learn about the opposite sex. It is an ongoing learning experience that is never completed. We will never know exactly what makes girls do the things they do, just as they will never fully understand what makes us do the things we do.

I have included the following two checklists for your use. The first should be used when preparing for a date, and the second should be used while on the date. Good luck, and I hope you meet the person of your dreams.

How to Prepare

[ ] Don't take a girl's number if you will not call
[ ] Call a new girl within two days of meeting her
[ ] Ask her out at least three days in advance
[ ] Work out
[ ] Dress well
[ ] Be informed
[ ] Eat well
[ ] If you are bald, don't hide it
[ ] Positive attitude
[ ] Trim your nose hairs

Brad Berkowitz

[ ] Shower, shave, shit
[ ] Change your sheets
[ ] Clean your apartment
[ ] Don't leave wine glasses in the sink
[ ] Barry White or Luther Vandross must be in your CD
  player
[ ] Have a bottle of white wine in the fridge
[ ] Make sure your answering machine volume is low
[ ] Be prompt
[ ] Plan on taking her out away from her place and your's

WHAT TO DO ON THE DATE

[ ] Pick her up at her place
[ ] Compliment her apartment
[ ] Don't call her again if you didn't enjoy the first date
[ ] Don't smoke cigarettes
[ ] Be careful when asking about ex-boyfriends
[ ] Listen to her when she talks
[ ] Be polite
[ ] Hold the door for her
[ ] Pay for the first few dates
[ ] Romance is important in relationships
[ ] Remember that girls really don't enjoy watching pornos
[ ] Take your time when it comes to having sex
[ ] Somehow determine her promiscuity
[ ] Go down on her
[ ] Stay the night after having sex
[ ] Call the day after having sex, especially when it is the
  first time

IX. Epilogue

The author of this book is currently writing a book comprised of people's worst or funniest dating experiences. By submitting a story, you agree that you will not be compensated in any way and agree to waive any recourse. Should you like to have your date considered for this upcoming book, please type and send a letter describing the date, along with your first name and hometown to:

Brad Berkowitz
P.O. Box 20507
New York, NY 10021-0069